John Thomas Micklethwaite

The ornaments of the rubric

John Thomas Micklethwaite

The ornaments of the rubric

ISBN/EAN: 9783741193095

Manufactured in Europe, USA, Canada, Australia, Japa

Cover: Foto ©Lupo / pixelio.de

Manufactured and distributed by brebook publishing software (www.brebook.com)

John Thomas Micklethwaite

The ornaments of the rubric

Alcuin Club Tracts.

I.

THE ORNAMENTS OF THE RUBRIC

BY

J. T. MICKLETHWAITE, F.S.A.

Thus saith the LORD, *Stand ye in the ways, and see, and ask for the old paths, where is the good way, and walk therein, and ye shall find rest for your souls.*
                                           Jeremiah vi. 16.

PRICE FIVE SHILLINGS

LONGMANS, GREEN, AND CO.
39 PATERNOSTER ROW, LONDON
NEW YORK AND BOMBAY
1897

[*All rights reserved*]

LONDON
HARRISON AND SONS, PRINTERS IN ORDINARY TO HER MAJESTY,
ST. MARTIN'S LANE.

TABLE OF CONTENTS.

ADVERTISEMENT BY THE COMMITTEE	5
PREFACE BY THE AUTHOR	7
LIST OF INVENTORIES AND AUTHORITIES	9
THE ORNAMENTS OF THE RUBRIC	13
APPENDIX ON THE ALTAR SHELF BY THE COMMITTEE	63
INDEX	65

ADVERTISEMENT BY THE COMMITTEE.

The Alcuin Club Tracts are issued under the direct supervision of the Committee; but the author of a tract, when it is published with his name, is alone responsible for the details.

In the present instance, many suggestions have been made in the course of the consideration of the Tract by the Committee, and some of these have been incorporated by the Author. The Tract may be said, in a general sense, though not in every detail, to represent the views of the Committee.

Author's Preface.

Some years since I wrote a paper on "The Literal Meaning of the Ornaments Rubric," for the St. Paul's Ecclesiological Society, and it was printed in the second volume of the Society's *Transactions*. The greater part of that paper was taken up by a descriptive catalogue of the ornaments found in parish churches in the second year of King Edward VI. On the formation of the Alcuin Club it seemed good to the Committee to issue such a catalogue, and I was asked to allow mine to be reprinted. I consented willingly, and the leave of the Executive of the St. Paul's Society was obtained. But when the Committee met to discuss the matter further, it was thought that it would be better to quote authorities more than had been done before, and I proposed to add some items to the list. As to the last, they are not important in their bearing on Church questions, but some are curious and interesting to the antiquary; and, as the wish has been to give as true a picture as possible of the contents of churches at the time under consideration, it seemed right to include them.

All the substance of the former paper remains, but the examples and authorities quoted are more than double what they were. They might have been increased indefinitely, and the sources from which they have been drawn might have been more various. But it is believed that no statement needing support is left without it, and if some authorities have been quoted rather often it is because they were ready at hand, and being good in themselves, will serve for matters of general use as well as a wider gathering would.

The difficulty has often been, not to find, but to select, the quotation. For some specially good ones I have to thank two of my colleagues on the Committee, Mr. Leland L. Duncan, F.S.A., and Mr. W. H. St. John Hope; and our Chairman, Dr. Wickham Legg, F.S.A., has helped much by pointing out where further illustration seemed to be required. At his suggestion a list of authorities is given.

J. T. M.

15, Dean's Yard, Westminster,
    3rd September, 1897.

LIST OF THE CHIEF INVENTORIES AND OTHER AUTHORITIES REFERRED TO IN THE PRESENT TRACT.

A worke entytled of ye olde god and the newe, London, John Byddell, 1534.

All Souls College, Oxford: Inventory in *Archæological Journal*, 1894. Vol. li. p. 120.

Archaeologia: the transactions of the Society of Antiquaries of London, 4to. Printed by Nichols & Sons. The *Proceedings* of the Society of Antiquaries are a different publication, in 8vo.

Archaeologia Cantiana: Transactions of the Kent Archæological Society: Printed by Mitchell & Hughes, London.

Berkshire, *see* Money, and *Ecclesiastical*.

Boston: *see* Peacock.

Bristol: *see* Nicholas.

Boys, William: *Collections for an history of Sandwich in Kent*, Canterbury, 1892. (*sic*, for 1792.)

Bury Wills: *Wills and Inventories from the registers of the commissary of Bury St. Edmund's and the Archdeacon of Sudbury*, ed. by Samuel Tymms, Camden Society, 1850. Vol. xlix.

Catterick: *see* Raine.

Christopher le Stocks, Saint, London: Inventory of 1488. *Archaeologia*, 1880. Vol. xlv. p. 111.

Crede Michi: see Wordsworth.

Derby, All Saints: J. C. Cox and W. H. St. John Hope, *The Chronicles of All Saints, Derby*, Lond. 1881.

Device for the Coronation of King Henry VII. in *Rutland Papers*, Camden Society, 1842.

Douthwaite, W. R.: *Gray's Inn*, Lond. 1886, second edition.

Durandus, Gulielmus: *Rationale Divinorum Officiorum*, Neapoli, Jos. Dura, 1859.

Durham: *Rites of Durham Abbey*, Surtees Society, 1842.

Dymond: *see* Petrock.

Ecclesiastical and Architectural Topography of England, (Berkshire), Archæological Institute, Oxford and London, John Henry Parker, 1849. No pagination. Goosey is described at paragraph 61.

Ecclesiologist, published by the Cambridge Camden Society, afterwards the Ecclesiological Society.

Exeter, Diocese of, Episcopal Registers of: ed. F. C. Hingeston-Randolph, in five volumes.

Exeter, Petrock, Saint: *see* Petrock.

Faversham: Inventory in *Archaeologia Cantiana*, 1889. xviii. 103.

Finchale, Priory of: see *Transactions of the Architectural and Archæological Society of Durham and Northumberland*, Durham, 1896. Vol. iv. p. 134.

Gairdner, J.: *Paston Letters*, Lond. 1874, in three volumes.

Gentleman's Magazine, London, 1755. Vol. xxv. p. 68.

Glasscock, J. L.: *The records of St. Michael's Parish Church, Bishop's Stortford*, London, Elliot Stock, 1882.

Great St. Mary's, Cambridge: *see* Sandars.

Hall, [Edward,] *The union of the two noble and illustre famelies of Lancastre and Yorke* [often called Hall's *Chronicle*]. 1548. Vol. ii. fol. lxxiii. verso. the xii.th year of Henry VIII.

Heales, Alfred: *The Early History of the Church of Kingston-upon-Thames*, London, 1883.

Hingeston-Randolph: *see* Exeter, Diocese of.

Holinshed, Raphael: *The Historie of England*, London, January 1587.

Illustrations of the Manners and Expences of antient times in England, Printed by John Nichols, London, 1797.

Injunctions: *see* Wilkins, D.: *Concilia*, Lond. 1737. vol. iii. and vol. iv.

Kerry, Charles: *A History of the Municipal Church of St. Lawrence, Reading*, Reading, 1883.

Lawrence, Saint, Reading: *see* Kerry.

Leverton, Churchwardens' accounts: in *Archaeologia*, 1867. Vol. xli. p. 333.

Liber Pontificalis Chr. Bainbridge, Archiepiscopi Eboracensis, Surtees Society, ed. Dr. Henderson, 1875.

Lincoln, 1548: *Archaeologia*, 1893. Vol. liii. p. 1. A paper by the Rev. Chr. Wordsworth on Inventories of Plate, Vestments &c. belonging to the Cathedral Church of the Blessed Mary of Lincoln.

Long Melford: *see* Neale.

Lyndewode, William: *Provinciale seu Constitutiones Anglic*, Lond. (printed at Antwerp) apud Franciscum Bryckman, 1525. Dec. 20.

Machyn: *Diary of Henry Machyn, Citizen and Merchant-Taylor of London*, Camden Society, 1848. Vol. 42.

Margaret Pattens, Saint, London: Inventories in *Archæological Journal*, 1885. Vol. xlii. p. 312.

Margaret, Saint, Westminster: Churchwardens' Accounts of, in *Illustrations of the Manners* &c. p. 1.

Mary at Hill, Saint, London: see *Illustrations of the Manners* &c. Nichols, p. 85.

Maydestone, Clement: *see* Wordsworth.

Michael, Saint, Cornhill, London: *The accounts of the Churchwardens of the Parish of St. Michael, Cornhill*, edited by William Henry Overall. Privately printed, (before 1871.)

Money, Walter: *Parish Church Goods in Berkshire*, A.D. 1552, Oxford and London, James Parker, 1879.

Myrc, John: *Instructions for parish priests*, Early English Text Society, 1868.

Neale, John Preston, and Le Keux, John: *Views of the most interesting Collegiate and Parochial Churches in Great Britain*, London, Longmans, 1824.

Nicholas, Saint, Bristol: *Proceedings of the Clifton Antiquarian Club for 1884-88*. Vol. i. p. 142.

Nichols: see *Illustrations*.

Norwich, St. Leonard's Priory: Inventory in *Norfolk Archaeology*, 1895. vol. xii. p. 196.

Oxford: *see* All Souls.

Parker, J. H.: see *The Ecclesiastical and Architectural Topography of England*, (Berkshire) 1849.

Peacock, Edward, *English Church Furniture*, London, 1866.

Peter Cheap, Saint, London: On the parish of, edited by the Rev. W. Sparrow Simpson in the *Journal of the British Archæological Association*, 1868. Vol. xxiv. p. 248.

Peter, Saint, Cornhill: *Antiquary* 1897. September and October, Vol. xxiii. pp. 278 and 312.

Petrock, Saint, Exeter, History of: Robert Dymond, *Report and Transactions of the Devonshire Association for the advancement of Science, Literature and Art*, Plymouth, Brendon & Sons, 1882. Vol. xix. p. 402.

Pontifical of Egbert, Archbishop of York, Surtees Society, 1853.

Privy Council: *see* Wilkins, D.: *Concilia*, Lond. 1737. vol. iii. and vol. iv.

Proceedings of the Society of Antiquaries of London, printed by Nichols.

Processionale ad usum insignis ac praeclarae Ecclesiae Sarum, Leeds, 1882. Ed. by Dr. Henderson.

Raine, James, *Catterick Church . . . contract for its building*, Lond. J. Weale, 1834.

Reading: *see* Kerry.

Ripon: see *Memorials of Ripon*, Surtees Society.

Sandars, Samuel, and Venables: *Historical and Architectural Notes on Great Saint Mary's Church Cambridge,* Cambridge, Antiquarian Society, 1869. Sold by Deighton, Bell, & Co.

Sandwich, Kent: *see* Boys.

Sarum Inventory of 1222: in Daniel Rock, *Church of our Fathers,* Lond. 1853. Vol. iii. Part ii. p. 99.

Scarborough, St. Mary's: Inventory in *Archaeologia,* 1888. li. 61.

Southampton, Austin Friars: *Hampshire Field Club, Papers and Proceedings,* No. iv. 1890. p. 20.

Stephen, Saint, Coleman Street, London: Inventory in *Archaeologia,* 1887. Vol. L p. 34.

Stephen Walbrook, Saint, London: *Transactions of the London and Middlesex Archæological Society,* Vol. v. 1881. p. 327.

Stephen's, Saint, Westminster: Inventory in the *Transactions of the London and Middlesex Archæological Society,* 1873. Vol. iv. p. 365.

Sussex Archæological Collections, published by the Sussex Archæological Society: Lewes, printed by Farncombe & Co.

Testamenta Eboracensia, Surtees Society, Part I. 1836. Part II. 1855.

Tyssen's Surrey Inventories: Daniel-Tyssen, John Robert, *Inventories of the Goods and Ornaments in the churches of Surrey,* reprinted from *Surrey Archæological Collections,* published by the Surrey Archæological Society, 1869. Vol. iv. p. 1.

Vert, Claude de, *Explication . . . . des Ceremonies de l'Église,* Paris, second ed. 1709, in four volumes.

Vetusta Monumenta, published by the Society of Antiquaries of London.

Westminster Abbey Inventories: At the suppression: *Transactions of the London and Middlesex Archæological Society,* 1873. Vol. iv. p. 313. In 1388: *Archaeologia,* 1890. Vol. lii. p. 213.

Wilkins, David: *Concilia,* Lond. 1737, in four volumes.

Wills: in MS. at Somerset House.

Wordsworth, Chr. *Tracts of Clement Maydestone,* Henry Bradshaw Society, 1894.

York Fabric Rolls: *The Fabric Rolls of York Minster,* Surtees Society, Vol. xxxv. 1859.

York Massbooks: *Missale ad usum insignis ecclesiae Eboracensis,* Surtees Soc. 1874. ed. by Dr. Henderson, i. 109.

Beyond the inventories that have been used in the present tract, there is a good catalogue of English inventories in Fernand de Mély and Edmund Bishop's *Bibliographie générale des Inventaires imprimés,* Paris, Ernest de Roux, 1893. The English inventories are in the first volume and in the first fasciculus of the second volume.

THE ORNAMENTS OF THE RUBRIC.

"*And here is to be noted, That such Ornaments of the Church, and of the Ministers thereof at all times of their Ministration, shall be retained, and be in use, as were in this Church of England, by the authority of Parliament, in the second year of the reign of King Edward the Sixth.*"

So runs the rubric in the Book of Common Prayer, which, after standing there neglected and almost forgotten for two hundred years, has in our time been brought very much into notice, and attempts to obey it have led to extravagances which are not only shocking to persons of refined taste, but sometimes not free from a tendency to suggest false teaching. The science of Ecclesiology, invented about half a century since, at a time of strong religious revival, soon attracted many enthusiastic disciples. But enthusiasm without study could not carry its subject very far. There have been a succession of real students from the beginning, but the sciolists have been the more numerous and perhaps the more aggressive, and when ecclesiological teaching became ecclesiastical practice the influence of the sciolists on its course was by far the greatest.

The result has been the setting up of the standard called *correctness* which has ruled the planning and the ornaments of churches for many years. *Correctness* has no definite principle underlying it, and it takes little notice of the adaptation of the buildings or their furniture to the uses for which they are intended. Several elements have contributed to its making. Reading had a little to do with it, a superficial knowledge of our own ancient churches rather more, and hints taken from modern practice in foreign churches most of all. These have been combined and modified by a sort of timidity which attempting compromise has often achieved monstrosity.

The timidity is now beginning to wear off, and the tendency towards outlandish novelties is increasing. The text books to which the clergy look for guidance prescribe things strange and modern as if they had the authority of the rubric, and without doubt many use them who would not if they did not so believe of them.

As a matter of taste this is deplorable, and as a matter of policy it is mischievous. The wish to make full use of the Prayer Book and what it orders comes of the increasing vitality of the Church. And the same cause has roused against her the more bitter hostility of the sects. She has to repel attacks from all sides, and can not without danger occupy an indefensible position.

The desire to add to the dignity of the surroundings of public worship beyond what was usual in our grandfathers' time is a right and proper one, and it will go on increasing. But as to ornaments it may be satisfied without going beyond the Book of Common Prayer. The intention of this present tract is to show what were the ornaments used at the time the rubric names, and it will be seen that it includes enough for the setting forth of a most ornate ceremonial, and some things besides, which perhaps no one would wish to revive now. The mention of such must not be understood as a recommendation of their use. But the things were in use at the time which fixes the law, and it would be very difficult to maintain that their presence in a church would now be unlawful. And certainly, if the usages with which any of them were connected should be restored without any new directions concerning them being given by proper authority, those ornaments and none other ought to be used.

In drawing up the list attention has been given especially to parish churches, but a few points have been noted wherein their arrangements imitated or differed from those of the cathedral and other collegiate churches, or *quires* as the rubric calls them.

We must begin by understanding clearly what are the limits of the enquiry. The rubric, which in its present form became part of the law of the Church and Realm of England in the year 1662, says that the ornaments to be retained and used are to be the same that were *in this Church of England, by the authority of Parliament, in the second year of the reign of King Edward the Sixth.* First, *in this Church of England:* not in the Church of France, or of Spain, or of Rome, or of Jerusalem, or any other;

nor in the Congregation of Geneva, or of Frankfort, or of Strasburg. Secondly, *by the authority of Parliament:* not by the authority of the King, or of the Privy Council, or of the Bishop of Rome, or of the Archbishop of Canterbury, or any other. And, thirdly, *in the second year of the reign of King Edward the Sixth:* not in the third, fourth, fifth, sixth or seventh year of that reign, nor in the reigns of Mary, Elizabeth, James I. or Charles I. The want of a clear understanding as to these three points has been the cause of many mistakes and much misunderstanding, and it will be well to consider them a little further.

I. THE CHURCH OF ENGLAND. We are referred to the usages of our own Church, and it is to documents concerning that Church that we must turn for information. It does not, however, follow that all study of foreign customs is useless. On the contrary, we should sometimes find it difficult to understand what is recorded of our own without it. But the help comes oftener from those local usages which the Roman policy has for centuries been trying to destroy than from the common form which it tries to enforce.

A few ornaments of foreign Protestant origin, such as the moveable bowl for use instead of the font, have at times obtained a place here; but as they are now generally given up, and they who used them would hardly have claimed the authority of the rubric for doing so, we need not stay to consider them.

II. THE AUTHORITY OF PARLIAMENT. Here I must first guard myself from anything which might seem like a contention that Parliament has of itself any power to regulate the ceremonial of the Church. Such would be an insult to the faith and the reason of Churchmen. I hope to show why the authority of Parliament at a given date was named as fixing the rule of the Church as to ornaments in 1662, as it had been before in 1559. And it is not necessary for us to enquire now whether the ruling of Parliament has always had constitutional authority; for, if anything were lacking before, it was certainly supplied, when, in 1662, there was put forth the present order, concerning the authority of which there can not be any dispute. But it needs to be remembered that we are referred to the authority of Parliament because the matter has been much obscured by the frequent quotation of other authorities whose orders, apart from the question of date, were not constitutionally binding upon the Church when they were issued, and have not been accepted by the Church and lawfully enacted afterwards, as, in this matter, the ruling of Parliament has been.

III. THE SECOND YEAR OF KING EDWARD THE SIXTH. King Henry VIII. died on the 28th day of January, 1547, and consequently the first regnal year of his son and successor began on 28th January, 1547, and ended on 27th January, 1548, and his second year on the corresponding days in 1548 and 1549. We have therefore to enquire what ornaments of the Church and of the ministers thereof were retained and used by authority of Parliament in the year which began on 28th January, 1548, and ended on 27th January, 1549.

It has generally been assumed that the rubric refers to the first Prayer Book of Edward VI. But an examination of the dates proves that this is not so. That book received the authority of Parliament on January 21st, 1549, which is indeed just within the second year of the King. But the time when it was to come into use is named in the Act itself, which orders that it shall be used on the Whitsunday following (June 9th, 1549.) or, if it might be had sooner, then three weeks after a copy had been procured. So that, even if the book could have been obtained within the remaining week of the second year, which is unlikely, it could not have been used by authority of Parliament before the third year of King Edward, and we must seek for something earlier. Now late in 1547 an Act (1st Edward VI. cap. 1.) had been passed, ordering the restoration of Communion in both kinds. No form was included in the Act, but on the 8th of March following, a form was put forth by proclamation. It is known as the *Order of Communion*, and perhaps it may be disputed whether technically it has the authority of Parliament. But the *Order* was approved by the Convocation of the Province of Canterbury, and it was considered at the time to receive its parliamentary authority from the Act 31st Henry VIII. cap. 8.

The *Order of Communion* was to come into use on Easter
Day, 1548, and it continued until it was superseded by
the English book of 1549. It was not an order for the
Celebration, but only for the *Communion*, and it was to be
inserted into the old Latin service, which was to go on as
before " without varying of any other rite or ceremony
of the Mass."[1] This at least is evidence of the continu-
ance, all through the second year of King Edward, of the
old Latin Mass and by consequence of the ornaments used
in that service. As a matter of fact the same ornaments,
or at least all of them which have been the subject of
controversy in late times, were also used with the English
service of 1549. But I think we may see a reason why
first in 1559 (so soon afterwards that the supposition of
mistake or accident is impossible) and again in 1662 it
was thought better to refer back to the time before
the introduction of the English service than to that
in which it was used. The reign of Edward VI. was one
of continual strife and change, and, when we are referred
to a particular date in it, it is as necessary to keep exactly
to that date, as it would be if we were referred to one
date during the French Revolution. The party of
innovation were in power, but at first they had to deal
with a strong opposition of Catholic reformers, who had
to be got rid of before they were able to carry out their
designs. This indeed they never did to the fullest of
their intention. But they went far enough to make
Englishmen accept with gladness the accession of Mary,
and the changes which came with it. I have said the old
ornaments were used with the new book, but almost from
its first publication other changes began to be made, and
as the innovators became stronger, they pressed forward
their measures with little regard to law or order. They
arbitrarily put down the use of ornaments, even whilst
the book ordering them was still in force, and soon they
replaced it by a book of their own in which the externals
of worship were reduced almost to the lowest possible.
In Queen Elizabeth's time it was intended to continue the
use of the ancient ornaments, and it was much simpler

[1] The *Order of Communion* was only to be used when there were communicants besides the priest, which was not yet a general custom; and it is likely that at many churches it was not used more than once or twice. At all other times the service would go on as of old.

and less likely to be misunderstood to refer to the last year of an unbroken usage of centuries, than to the first year of a period of quick and often violent change. And where so many and contradictory orders had been made by all kinds of authority, scarce one of which had been used in a strictly constitutional way, it is difficult to see how any better course could have been taken, than to accept only those which had received the sanction of Parliament. The rule was at least a definite one, and if it had been fairly acted upon, it would probably have worked well; but the earlier bishops of Queen Elizabeth's time never honestly accepted it. They would have had things put back to what they were on the death of Edward, and failing to procure that by lawful means, they tried to obtain their end by acts of their own, as arbitrary as those of the Crown had ever been. Thus began that difference between the law and the practice of the English Church, which has not yet ceased. Much was recovered in the seventeenth century. Laud lost his life, but his cause was won. At the Restoration, the still existing, but generally neglected law, was deliberately re-enacted. Much was done towards putting it into practice then, and the way was prepared for that fuller revival, which after two more centuries, we see now. And it must be borne in mind, that, as in 1662 the standard of 1548 was returned to, any changes, which may have been made between these dates, were overruled, and deprived of any legal force which for the time being they may have had.

The present rubric then orders the use of the same ornaments as were in the year 1548. And we have seen that, so far as regards the Altar service, these ornaments were what had been used for many years before. This is true, also, with respect to other services. For although the Court party were attempting, in irregular ways, to put down usages connected with particular days, such as the giving of ashes on Ash Wednesday, and of palms on Palm Sunday, it was not done "by authority of Parliament," nor was anything done which materially affected the regular daily services, or the offices contained in the Manual, or any of the ornaments connected with them, before the appearance of the book of 1549.

The changes as to ornaments which had taken place up to the second year of King Edward, had reference not to the public services and regular ordinances of the Church, but to various usages which had grown up in the course of centuries, and which, innocent perhaps in their first beginning, had become superstitious abuses, and from the date of the definite rejection of the authority of the Bishop of Rome in this realm, efforts were made to put an end to them. They arose out of the worship of relics and images, and the various orders about them were summed up and repeated in the *Injunctions* issued by the Privy Council in 1547. These Injunctions depend for their Parliamentary authority on the Act 31st Henry VIII. cap. 8. already referred to as giving the authority to the *Order of Communion*. That Act gave the authority of Parliament, under certain restrictions, to Royal proclamations, and, during a minority, to proclamations issued by the Privy Council. It may be disputed whether this really does give the authority of Parliament within the meaning of the Act of Uniformity of 1662. But it would take me away from my subject to discuss that point, and I will assume that it does so. The *Injunctions* are a re-edition of a set which had been issued by Thomas Cromwell a dozen years before, and they contain little that was new in 1547. All relics, shrines, and everything connected with them were taken away, and all images which had been abused by offerings and other superstitious observances; also all pictures which recorded "feigned miracles." Lights were no longer to be set before any such nor elsewhere in the church, except two before the Sacrament of the Altar. This would make a considerable difference in the appearance of the churches; for although many might not possess shrines or relics, there was none in the land which did not possess at least one image before which it had been customary to burn a lamp, and some had many.

The confiscation of the property of guilds and chantries under 37th Henry VIII. cap. 4. seems only to have partly taken effect, and it was some years after its re-enactment by 1st Edward VI. cap. 14. before the work was complete. Beyond the taking away of the lights which most guilds had kept up, the effect upon the ornaments of the Church was very little. The ornaments which had been used at the private services were of the same sort as those which continued to be used in the public services. In a few, chiefly of the largest, churches there were altars which had been built only for the use of chantries, and would now be left desolate. But by far the largest number of churches had none such, the chantries, if there were any, being founded at public altars.[1]

The Injunctions forbid certain uses of bells, and order the setting up in every church of a copy of the great Bible and the *Paraphrases* of Erasmus, in some place where the parishioners could read them; and that a pulpit should be provided in every church that did not already possess one.

The list of ornaments in the second year of King Edward the Sixth is, then, a list of such as would have been found in a church of the beginning of the sixteenth century, with certain omissions and certain additions due to these various enactments. Such a list I now endeavour to give. I can not hope that nothing will be left out of it, but I will try that nothing shall be put into it for which reasonable proof can not be given.

The sources of our information are many and much scattered. Not much can be got from the old service books, except with respect to what are now called occasional offices. A knowledge of the customs and ceremonial of the ordinary services was assumed in the users of the books. I think I am right in saying that in no old English Mass book is there more mention of the altar lights than there is in the Prayer Book of 1662.[2] But much can be learned from the various constitutions and ordinations whereby it was ruled how the duty of providing the requisite ornaments should be divided between

---

[1] It has been, and still is, the custom of careless or ignorant writers to call all side altars *chantry* altars. But many of them never had chantries founded at them, and, generally, where there was a chantry, the altar was there long before the foundation. A chantry means an endowment and not an altar or a chapel.

[2] This by itself is enough to upset the contention that the absence of express mention of a thing in an office book is proof of its non-use. And for the continuation of the old tradition until after the year 1548 it is enough to cite the rubric of the book of 1549, which directs that the priest preparing for Mass shall put on *the vesture appointed for that ministration*. But where appointed, except by immemorial usage? There had not been any new order about the vestments.

the parishioners, the rectors, and the vicars of churches.[1] Much, too, may be gleaned from the records of visitations and from old wills. And, most of all, from the churchwardens' accounts, the minutes of parish meetings, the inventories of church goods, and from the evidence afforded by the old churches themselves.[2] It would be tedious to cite authority for each single object, but I shall try to do it wherever the obscurity or curiosity of the matter seems to ask for it.

To take the ornaments of the church first:

IMAGES AND PICTURES. The church might be decorated with these on walls, in windows, or on furniture, if only they did not commemorate feigned miracles and were not abused by superstitious practices, but were "for a memorial only." Several irregular attempts have been

---

[1] The rule as to the parishioners' share was laid down for the province of Canterbury by a constitution of Archbishop Robert Winchelsea in 1305, which may well be quoted at length here as the evidence of the use of many of the things which will be mentioned later:

"*Ut parochiani ecclesiarum singularum nostre Cantuariensis provincie sint decetero certiores de defectibus ipsos contingentibus, ne inter rectores et ipsos ambiguitas generetur temporibus successivis, volumus decetero et precipimus quod teneantur invenire omnia inferius annotata, videlicet, legendas, antiphonarium, gradale, psalterium, troperium, ordinale, missale, manuale, calicem, vestimentum principale cum casula dalmatica tunica et cum capa in choro cum omnibus suis appendiciis, frontale ad magnum altare cum tribus tuellis, tria superpellicia, unum rochetum, crucem processionalem, crucem pro mortuis, thuribulum, lucernam, tintinabulum ad deferendum coram corpore Christi in visitatione infirmorum, pixidem pro corpore Christi, honestum velum quadragesimale, vexilla pro rogationibus, campanas cum chordis, feretrum pro defunctis, vas pro aqua benedicta, osculatorium, candalabrum pro cereo paschali, fontem cum serura, imagines in ecclesia, imaginem principalem in cancello, clausuram cimiterii, reparationem navis ecclesie interius et exterius tam in imaginibus quam in fenestris vitreis, reparationem librorum et vestimentorum quandocunque contigerit eadem reparationibus indigere. Cetera autem omnia tam in reparatione cancelli quam in aliis hic non expressis secundum diversas consuetudines approbatas a locorum rectoribus et vicariis seu ad quos pertinet habent in omnibus reparari sumptus eorundem.*"

(Lyndewode, *Provinciale, Lib. III. De ecclesiis edificandis* cap. ii. fo. clxxxi.*b*.)

This constitution though modified to some degree by local customs, as diocesan orders printed by Wilkins and others show, gives us generally what obligations were laid upon the parishioners. The respective shares of the parsons and the vicars were not so uniform, and must be sought in each case in the ordination deed whereby the vicarage was constituted and wherein the division of the profits and the burdens of the Ienefice is generally set forth in detail.

[2] Some information may be gathered from contemporary literature, and especially from controversial literature, but more about ceremonial and customs than about the ornaments. Anyone with patience to wade through the scurrilous profanity of a writer like Thomas Becon may find a great deal. But such writers need to be used with caution. Their teaching was foreign and their writing contains much which is translated, and in which the references and allusions are to foreign customs. Barnabe Googe's *Popish Kingdom* is of this sort, and the large use made of it in Brand's *Popular Antiquities* is very misleading, for most of the extravagances attacked were never practised in England.

made to stop the use of images and pictures as church ornaments, but it was never formally forbidden and never quite given up in England.[1] The series known as the *Stations of the Cross* is both foreign and modern. It was only introduced into English churches about thirty years since.

THE HIGH ALTAR. This was of stone, as were other altars.[2] The very few examples of wooden altars in England during the later middle ages were irregular and contrary to the canons in force at the time.[3] The destruction of the old altars and the substitution of moveable wooden tables, which seem to have been set up only at the time of the Celebration of the Eucharist, appear to have been begun in the diocese of London by Dr. Ridley in the fourth year of King Edward.[4]

MINOR ALTARS. Even the smallest of parish churches

---

[1] Even when the ideal of a church was a square box, with a central pulpit in three stories, and galleries and close pews all round, it was common to set up pictures, often crucifixes, over the altars. One such, about a hundred years old, remains in St. John's Church, Wakefield; and another a few years more recent in the neighbouring church of Thornes.

[2] Our old English altars did not always have relics enclosed in them. Lyndewode in his *Provinciale*, Lib. iii. commenting on the words *loco reliquiarum* in the title *De reliquiis et veneratione sanctorum*, does say that altars should not be consecrated without relics; but he adds "*si tamen consecretur altare sine reliquiis tenet consecratio.*" (fo. clxxx.) And the wording of the rubrics in the Pontificals seems to show that this use of relics was the exception rather than the rule.

[3] There can be no doubt that wooden altars were sometimes used in England in the fifteenth and sixteenth centuries, and they not mere makeshifts, but things of some cost. In 1435 Richard Russell, citizen and merchant of York, amongst other bequests to his parish church, St. John Baptist's, Hungate, in that city, willed "*quod unum altare fiat bene et effectualiter de tabulis in parte boreali dictae ecclesiae, coram ymaginibus Beatae Mariae et Sanctae Annae, et subtus idem altare unum almarriolum pro libris et vestimentis eidem altari pertinentibus fideliter conservandis. Et quod unum aliud altare fiat sufficienter ex parte australi dictae ecclesiae coram ymaginibus Sanctarum Katerinae & Mariae Magdalenae secundum formam alterius altaris supradicti.*" (*Test. Ebor.* ii. 53.) At St. Peter's Cornhill "an old awter of wood w[t] other olde lumber" was sold between Michaelmas 1549, and Michaelmas 1551. (p. 312.)

[4] The real contest in the seventeenth century was not about the material so much as the position of the altar, and that was finally set at rest after 1662. Stone or marble altars of the eighteenth and the first half of the nineteenth century are not uncommon. There will be occasion to mention one or two later on. In 1891 I saw one in the church of Long Clawson in Leicestershire which was curious for its classical affectation. It was only 3 feet 9 inches long, was of solid stone consisting of a die with a moulded plinth and cap after the Roman pagan manner, and it bore in front a dedicatory inscription *Deo Triuno Optimo Maximo* with the date 1738. Altars set up in the better sort of churches during the eighteenth century had generally marble tops, which were often carried by ironwork fixed into the wall or the floor. Examples of this were very common till lately; but now many have been taken away, and amongst them those of the old church, now the cathedral, at Wakefield, St. Mary's Church, Beverley, and All Saints' Church, Derby.

appear to have had two altars, besides the high altar. Churches without aisles or transepts had the minor altars one on each side of the chancel door.[1] Five altars seems to have been a very usual number in parish churches of the better sort, and collegiate and cathedral churches had many more, as may often be seen by the marks of them which remain. These altars were still in regular use in 1548. The introduction of the new book in 1549 did not at first make any difference in this respect. The old services were kept on at the old times and in the old places, the English form being used instead of the Latin.[2]

THE TABLE, OR REREDOS. Sometimes there was a wall or screen of wood or stone behind the altar, covered with imagery and painting, and sometimes it had shutters or "leaves" to close it in.[3]

THE ALTAR SHELF.[4] In earlier times the ornaments of the

---

[1] The beautiful reredoses of two altars thus placed remain at Ranworth Church, Norfolk, and the altars themselves at Partrishow Church, Brecon.

[2] A Privy Council Order, of 24th June, 1549, orders the discontinuance of "Our Lady's Communion" and the "Apostles' Communion," kept in the chapels of St. Paul's, and directs that, in future, only one Communion shall be kept, at the time of High Mass, except there were some who desired to receive at another time. For them a special celebration was allowed, but it was to be at the High Altar. As late as 1567 the churchwardens of Kingston, in Surrey, made three new Communion tables of wood for their church, which already had one, so there were four. "Remayn in the cherch the iiij. comunyon tables that thes yer were new mayd; (that is, to say) in the hey chancell, j in Syntt Jamys chancell & on in Trenyte chancell; & the other old table also remanyng." (*The Early History of the Church of Kingston-upon-Thames*, by Major Alfred Heales, p. 85.) These tables seem to have taken the places of as many old stone altars. Henry the Seventh's altar in the Lady Chapel, at Westminster Abbey, stood until the Puritan usurpation, and there is evidence of services at it. The rubrics of the coronation service still assume the existence of the altar of St. Edward at Westminster Abbey. The Lady Chapels of Winchester and Gloucester Cathedrals have (unless they have been taken away lately) altar rails of the seventeenth century, the former being, I think, earlier than 1662, and the other later.

[3] See a description of the Church of Melford, in Suffolk, by Mr. Roger Martin, who remembered it as it was at the date we are discussing. It is printed in Neale's *Views of Churches*, Vol. II. William Boston of Newark, chaplain (1467,) left forty shillings by will to the altar of the Holy Trinity in the church of Newark, adding "*et volo quod ista summa expendatur in honesta clausura biforali circa tabulam ad altare predictum.*" (*Test. Ebor.* ii. 283.) I believe this altar was in the south transept of the church. At Haconby in Lincolnshire in 1562, amongst other things, they destroyed "one greate alter table w⁴ leaves full of Imagies of allablaster." (Peacock's *Church Furniture*, p. 94.)

[4] Some of my colleagues on the committee of the Alcuin Club, arguing only from negative evidence, contend that the altar shelf was not used in England until modern times. As they have not been able to convince me, nor I them, they are to state their view in a separate note. And I prefer to leave what I had written with only a few verbal corrections, and the addition of this further note. I suppose my friends will not dispute that the altar shelf was used before the middle of the sixteenth century in France, Germany and the Low Countries, and, if so, it is at the least

altar generally stood directly upon it. But towards the end of the middle ages there had grown up a custom of putting them, in parish churches especially, upon a ledge or shelf, either set upon the altar or behind it. We find it mentioned by many names. An inventory of goods belonging to the Church of St. Stephen, Coleman Street, mentions *iiij Coffyns to ly on the auters*,[1] which I believe were altar shelves in the form of long wooden boxes. Another inventory of goods belonging to the Church of St. Mary at Hill, in 1485, records *a frontell for the schelffe standyng on the altar*.[2] One three years later of the goods of the Church of St. Christopher le Stocks, has a *forme uppon the high alter undre the juellis*, and Holinshed,[3] describing Henry VIII.'s Chapel on the Field of the Cloth of Gold, mentions the thing as an *halpas* and again as a *deske*. The destruction of ancient altars has been so general that the survival of any number of altar shelves is not to be expected, but a few examples remain. At Grantham Church in Lincolnshire, in a crypt below the south chancel aisle, there still stands an old altar, and behind the slab is a low and quite plain shelf of stone. And at Cold Overton Church in Leicestershire at the east end of the south aisle, where once an altar stood, its shelf remains attached to the wall. The front of it is decorated with carving. There is preserved in Romsey Abbey Church a painted table or reredos of the time of Henry VII. or a little later, and the lower part of it bears clear marks of a shelf, probably in the form of a wooden box, having been placed before it.[4]

---

probable that it would not be unknown in England. I have never maintained that its use was general here. The conservative Abbeys and Colleges may have kept, and very likely did keep, to the older fashion, and many of the country parishes probably did the same. But the passages given above and others like them leave to me no doubt that the shelf was often used in the better appointed town parish churches. Perhaps they may have got it from the friars. The word *halpas*, like the French *gradine*, means a *step*, and the attempt to explain the object so called into an upstanding "table" or reredos is too violent to be convincing.

[1] *Archaeologia*, 1887. Vol. l. p. 44.

[2] Nichols's *Illustrations of Manners and Expenses*, p. 113.

[3] *The Historie of England*, Vol. iii. part ii. p. 857, edit. 1587.

[4] The altar shelf, like many other things, is sometimes made offensive by vulgar exaggeration, as when it is raised excessively high or developed into something like a flight of stairs. But used reasonably it is a seemly ornament to the altar, and one not to be condemned. Enough has been said in the text to show that it has the authority of the rubric, and its modern use is not altogether the revival of a thing obsolete. In the time of Charles I. a long cushion sometimes took the place of the shelf at the back of the altar, but that custom

THE CANOPY OF THE ALTAR. An altar often had above it a canopy of cloth, wood, or other material. The view of the presbytery of Westminster Abbey in the Islip roll[1] shows a canopy over the high altar, and there are some remains of that above the chantry altar within the grate of the tomb in Henry VII.'s Chapel. A wooden canopy still exists at Clun Church, Salop, but the "restorer" has had it down and refixed it to suit his "restoration" of the East end. Another is recorded to have remained over the altar at Goosey Church, Berkshire, till about fifty years ago.[2] In the chapel of the hospital at Sherborne, Dorset, there remain projecting from the east wall high up above the altar two long iron bars ending in shields. These once carried a canopy either of wood or of cloth on a wooden frame. The canopy on pillars does not seem to have been common here in the sixteenth century, but it was not unknown. There was one in Henry VII.'s Chapel, which remained with the altar beneath it until 1643.

THE HAIR. This was a covering of hair cloth to lay on the top of an altar.[3] I am not sure that it was always used.

THE UPPER FRONTAL OR DORSAL. A cloth of more or less richness hung against the wall above the altar.

---

does not seem to have survived the civil wars, whereas the older shelf did, and continued in use in some places until the revival came. There is a very pretty example at St. John's church, Wakefield, which was consecrated in 1796. It is of marble and stands upon an altar also of marble. And above it is the large picture of the Crucifixion, already mentioned. A still later, and perhaps the latest, case that can be attributed to the old tradition before the new revival began, was the high altar of Westminster Abbey, as it was before the present altar was set up in 1867. It was built about 1824, and was a block of artificial stone and black marble in the Gothic of the school of the Wyatts; and upon it stood a shelf of wood in the box form with, if I remember right, the middle part raised a few inches higher than the ends.

[1] *Vetusta Monumenta*, Vol. IV. Plate xviii. The engraving shews the canopy over the altar correctly, but the tower-like structure below it is a mistake of the copier, who has misinterpreted the representation of the veiled pyx hanging with its own canopy of three crowns beneath the flat canopy of the altar. The original drawing, in the possession of the Society of Antiquaries of London, is a good deal rubbed in that place.

[2] It is thus described by Mr. J. H. Parker in *The Ecclesiastical and Architectural Topography of England (Berkshire)* (1849): "over the altar, a flat P[erpendicular] tester is painted with emblems of the Crucifixion, &c.; and above this, on the east wall, a painting of the Crucifixion." It must have been taken away soon after Mr. Parker's visit, for in the *Ecclesiologist*, 1851. Vol. xii. p. 436, it is said that it "disappeared no one knows how" a few years before 1851. Enquiries about it kindly made for me by the Rev. O. Birchall resulted only in the information that nothing is remembered of it at Goosey now.

[3] "iiij. heeris to lay upon the alters." (St. Christopher le Stocks 1488, p. 116.)

THE NETHER OR LOWER FRONTAL.[1] The cloth in front of the altar to which the name *frontal* is now generally given.

THE FRONTLET was a strip of stuff fringed on the lower edge and sewn as an "apparel" on to the front edge of one of the linen cloths, from which it hung so as to hide the suspension of the lower frontal. It was not always used. The modern so-called *superfrontal*, which covers the top of the altar and hangs over in front, is contrary to the old custom, which placed only white linen on the top of the altar at the time of Mass.

ALTAR COVER. It has often been said that altars used to be vested only at the time of Mass. And this is very likely true as to some of the less important ones which were not often used. But it certainly was not always so; and as now a cover used to be provided to protect the vested altar from dust.[2]

THE ELEVATION CURTAIN. In 1508 the churchwardens of St. Lawrence's Church, Reading, paid a penny " for a carpynters lyne to draw the black sarsenet before the sacrament at the Hy Aulter."[3] In 1518 they of St. Peter's Church, Cheap, London, put down in their inventory " a clothe for the levacyon tyme with the pictur of the crucifix."[4] And in 1521 they of Leverton, in Lincolnshire, who had lately been setting up a new table or reredos to their high altar, paid " for iij quarters of blake tuyke to hyng betwyx the tabull of y⁶ hye auter and y⁶ sacrament at sacrye tyme and a lyne to y⁶ same, ix.d. ob."[5] These passages refer to a custom of the existence of which

---

[1] *Frontale ad magnum altare* was amongst the things to be found by the parishioners, and old pictures of English altars in use always shew them vested. The frontal might take the form of a tablet such as the well known example in Westminster Abbey, but I think it rarely did so in a parish church. There is no English authority for the altar itself being carved and painted. Most old ones were quite plain, but a few were panelled in front; as, for instance, that in William of Wykeham's chapel in the cathedral church of Winchester. The covering of the altar with "a carpet of silk or other decent stuff" at the time of service was ordered in the canons of 1603 which set forth the least in the way of ornaments which might be tolerated.

[2] " Also upon the auter lythe alweye an olde yelowe clothe of sylke, for to kepe alle the clothis clene that lyne on the auter" (St. Stephen's Walbrook c. 1480). " Four Cloths to lay upon the Altar[s], of black buckram." (Long Melford, p. 18. 1529.)

[3] *A history of the Church of St. Lawrence, Reading*, by the Rev. Charles Kerry, p. 26.

[4] Dr. Sparrow Simpson in the *Journal of the British Archæological Association*, 1868. xxiv. 259. The printers have blundered *levation* into *lenation*.

[5] Mr. Edward Peacock in *Archæologia*, xli. 348.

in England there is no other known evidence. And yet the distance of the three churches from one another shows that it must have been widely spread.[1] No rubric mentions it, and it does not survive amongst the popular customs of any country in Europe, and our text books are silent about it. But it did survive even to the eighteenth century in some French churches where, as Dom. Claude de Vert tells us,[2] they used to spread a small curtain or veil of violet or black above the middle of the altar just opposite the priest at the time of the elevation. The common explanation was that it was intended to make the Sacrament more easily seen by the worshippers when It was lifted up. But it is more likely that it came of a feeling that in the presence of the Sacrament imagery should be veiled. The fact that the evidence of this curtain in England is that by chance some small items about it have been entered in some churchwardens' books, which by chance have escaped destruction, and that three gentlemen who have published extracts from these books have by chance copied out those passages, should make us very careful not to reject a thing only for want of evidence about it. If our near neighbours had it, it is most likely that we had also.

THE CURTAINS, RIDDELS, OR COSTERS. It was usual to have curtains generally of light stuff hung at the ends of altars from rods projecting from the east wall, and at right angles with it. They are often mentioned in inventories by these names.[3]

CARPETS were laid on floors and on seats,[4] and

TAPESTRIES hung against walls of such churches as could afford them.[5]

---

[1] Since the above was written, Mr. St. John Hope, whom I have to thank for several other references, has sent me an extract from the parish accounts of St. Michael's Cornhill, for 1459, which gives another London example of the elevation curtain "for wyre a strynge and werekemanshepe for a litell clothe of Bokeram atte high awtor xij.d." (p. 17.)

[2] *Explication . . . des Cérémonies de l'Église,* (Paris, 1713,) Vol. IV. pp. 30-33.

[3] "A ffronte and a nether ffront for the high awter of rode silk with Swannys of gold and ij Curtoyns of rode silk." (St. Margaret Pattens, London, 1470, p. 316.)

[4] "Payed . . . for amendyng of the fote clothe that lieth afore the high Auter iijs." (St. Michael Cornhill, London, 1467, p. 35.) Sometimes skins were used. The parish church of Boston had in 1552 "ij polles to lye afore of aulter." (Peacock, p. 221.) They were sold for thirteen shillings and fourpence the following year.

[5] "A Grete cloth of Tapestri werke for to hang uppon the Walle by hynde the Sepulcur." (St. Margaret Pattens 1470, p. 319.)

THE HANGING PYX. THE CANOPY OF THE PYX. THE PYX CLOTH. The blessed Sacrament was reserved in English churches all through the year we are concerned with, and the old English way of doing it was by suspension over the high altar. A pulley or a sort of crane was fixed there with gear for raising and lowering, and the pyx was hung by a cord or chain attached to a ring on its top.[1] Above it was hung the canopy, a round tent-shaped thing of linen or silk, kept in form by a metal ring, and sometimes highly ornamented.[2] The pyx itself was veiled in the pyx cloth, which was a square napkin, with a hole in the middle through which the suspending cord passed, and weighted tassels at the four corners which kept it down close by the pyx.[3] The constitution of Archbishop Peckham in 1260, given in a note below,[4] seems to apply

[1] At West Grinstead church in Sussex there remains, in the chancel roof above the altar, a wooden lever hung on its middle, but thicker and therefore heavier at one end than the other. The pyx was suspended by a cord from the lighter end and lifted by the weight of the other. It is figured in the *Sussex Archæological Collections*, 1892. xxxviii. opposite p. 56. The altar canopy at Clun already mentioned had a pulley fixed below it for the suspension of the pyx. The great stone crown projecting from the top of the reredos of the high altar at Winchester Cathedral was to canopy the pyx and bears marks of the cords by which it was raised and lowered. There was a like arrangement at Christchurch in Hampshire and at St. Alban's Abbey, but it has been mutilated in each.

[2] In 1500 money was left to the church of Walberswick for, amongst other things, "a canope over the hygh awter, welle done with oure Lady and 4 aungelys and the Holy Ghost goyng upp and down with a cheyme." (Nichols's *Illustrations of Ancient Manners and Expenses*, p. 187.) "A canapy for the sacrament of crymson sarcenett with knoppis of golde and tacellys of sylke." (Inventory of goods belonging to Faversham church in 1512, printed in *Archæologia Cantiana*, xviii. 109.)

[3] Probably the only old English pyx cloth which remains was found some years since with a corporas case in the church chest of Hessett, Suffolk, by the late Canon, William Cooke, who described it thus in a letter to me: "It is square measuring on each side 2 feet 5½ inches. It is made of linen and worked into a pattern resembling lace by the drawing out of some threads and the knotting of others. Around it is a silk fringe of rose and yellow colours one inch in width, the colours alternating in spaces of an inch and a half. At one corner a gilt ball is still appended with a tassell of silk of the same colours as the fringe. The other balls, three in number, have become detached. In the centre is a round hole, in diameter more than an inch, bound with silk ribbon that shows a quarter of an inch on each side." See *Ecclesiologist*, 1868. xxix. 80.

[4] "Dignissimum eukaristie sacramentum precipimus decetero taliter custodiri ut in qualibet ecclesia parochiali fiat tabernaculum cum clausura decens et honestum secundum cure magnitudinem et ecclesie facultates in quo ipsum Dominicum Corpus non in bursa vel loculo propter comminutionis periculum nullatenus collocetur, sed in pixide pulcherrima lino candidissimo interius adornata, ita quod sine omni diminutionis periculo facile possit extrahi et imponi." On this Lyndewood remarks: "Videtur quod usus observatus in Anglia, ut scilicet in canapeo pendeat super altare, non est commendabilis." And again: "Licet enim consuetudo anglicana commendabilis sit illa consideratione qua citius representatur nostris aspectibus adoranda, non tamen est commendabilis eo respectu quo ponitur in loco publico, sic quod ad eam manus temerarie de facili valeant extendi. Nam, licet in cupa

rather to a locker than to a hanging canopy; but it is evident from Lyndewode's curious gloss that he did not know of any method of reservation in use here except suspension. There is, however, some small evidence of the occasional use of a locker over the high altar. In 1466 the church of St. Stephen, Coleman Street, London, had "j coffyn for to keep the sacrament ofi (?) the hy auter."[1] In 1547, as appears by their accounts, the churchwardens of St. Margaret's, Westminster, paid for the making of "a little coffer upon the hie altar for to set in the sacrament with other necessaries 1s. 4d."[2] The Austin friars of Southampton had at the suppression of their house "in the myddes of the auter a proper frame gylt for the sacrament."[3] And much earlier than any of these we find in the accounts of the keepers of the fabric of Ripon Minster for 1399–1400, "in salario Joh. Memersmyth emendantis j seram de cista in qua Corpus Christi ponitur, 3d."[4] Here *cista* seems scarcely to apply to the hanging pyx, though the hanging pyx was in some way secured by a lock.

LAMPS. The injunctions of 1547 order the retention of *two lights upon the high altar before the Sacrament*. It has generally been assumed that this refers to the candles placed upon the altar at the time of Mass, but a comparison of these injunctions with the earlier ones of

que forsan clausa est pendeat, tamen ad illam deorsum mittendam vel forsan cum illa cupa totaliter auferendam manus temerarie de facile possunt apponi. Et ideo, ut michi videtur, commendabilior est usus aliorum locorum quem vidi, vis.: in Hollandia et Portugalia in quibus ordinatur unus locus singularis honestus prope altari in quo reponitur eukaristia sub clavibus infra parietes, vel locum bene munitum, conservanda, sic quod nullus ad ipsam eukaristiam accedere poterit, nisi sacerdos loci illius clavem custodiens." (*Provinciale*, Lib. iii. *De custodia eukaristie* Cap. *Dignissimum*, fo. clxxix.) I do not know the ancient usage of Portugal, but from the way it is here spoken of it was probably the same as that of Holland, where the Sacrament was reserved, not in the Italian manner, but in a "sacrament house," on the north side of the presbytery. The same custom existed in Scotland in the sixteenth century, and I have sometimes doubted whether those often highly enriched lockers, which we find on the north sides of the chancels in the east of England, and which are called Easter Sepulchres, may not have been used for the reservation of the Sacrament. In Peacock's *English Church Furniture* (p. 80) it is recorded that the sepulchre at Ewerby, in Lincolnshire, was "broken in peces," but the stone locker is there yet. If, however, the lockers are "tabernacles," it is strange that Lyndewode should not have known of them, for most are as old as the fourteenth century. There is evidence of the use of the Italian tabernacle in some English churches in Mary's time, but it was not general.

[1] *Archaeologia*, 1887. l. p. 44.
[2] Nichols's *Illustrations of Ancient Manners and Expenses*, p. 12.
[3] *Hampshire Field Club, Papers and Proceedings*, No. iv. 1890, p. 20.
[4] *Memorials of Ripon*, edited by the Rev. J. T. Fowler for the *Surtees Society*, iii. 129.

Thomas Cromwell seems to prove that the lights intended to be kept were those before the reserved Sacrament, which were lights burning continually. These lights would continue in use so long as the Sacrament continued to be reserved. And there is no doubt that It was reserved all through the year 1548 and something beyond. Either wax or oil was burned in the lamps according to convenience. The hanging bason was perhaps the commonest form of lamp here, but brackets projecting from the wall were used, and sometimes we find a lampstead in a wall in the form of a niche, generally with a sort of hood above to catch the smoke, and less often with a small flue to carry it away.[1]

THE LINEN ALTAR CLOTHS. These seem to have varied in number from two to four, three perhaps being the most usual. The frontlet was sometimes sewn to the edge of one of them, as was said before. The topmost cloth was of as fine texture as could be afforded, and was often fringed and embroidered. It hung down at the ends, besides covering the top of the altar. Weights of lead were used to keep the altar vestments in their places.[2]

THE ALTAR CROSS. A cross was not thought a necessary ornament for an altar, though it was a common one. The cross which a parish was bound to provide was for processions. But often it served for the altar as well, being fitted with a foot to stand in, and a staff for carrying.[3] This cross generally had a figure of our Lord crucified,

---

[1] At Buscot church, near Lechlade, is a good example of the lampstead without flue, in the east jamb of the window, the sill of which forms the sedilia. It is of the thirteenth century. At Meppershall, Bedfordshire, is one with the flue, in the north wall of the chancel. At Tallington church, Lincolnshire, and Castor, Northamptonshire, both near to Peterborough, are two very curious examples, the former of the twelfth century and on the south side of the chancel, the other of the fourteenth century and on the north side. Each has a flue above, and a pierced bason in the bottom of the niche as if to drain away spilled oil. The flues are generally very small.

[2] "iij pila plumbi super altare, ad firmanda tualla." (Inventory of goods of the church of St. Kerrian, Exeter, 1417, printed by the Rev. F. C. Hingeston-Randolph as an appendix to his *Register of Edmund Stafford*, p. 483.) " j coveryng w^t iiij pecis of leed lying of the alter." (Inventory of goods belonging to a chantry in York Minster 1543. *York Fabric Rolls*, 283.) "*vj plumbetts rotundi inclusi corio. Item v plumbetts longi super altare.*" (St. Leonards priory, Norwich 1453. *Norfolk Archæology*, 1895. xii. 214.)

[3] The bede roll of St. Mary's, Sandwich, recorded the benefactions of John Colwyn and his wife, who gave "the best crosse of syluer and gylt with a staf of laton ther to, the whyche cost xxv^{li}." and also of Thomas Grene and his wife and John Byschop, who gave "the fote of syluer for that crosse to stand ther on the hygh auter." (Boys's *Sandwich*, p. 373.)

and sometimes there were brackets at the sides with figures of St. Mary and St. John.[1]

THE ALTAR CANDLESTICKS. The direction in the *Order of Communion* that the old service should continue without varying of any rite or ceremony, sends us back to the ancient usage as to altar lights. This differed much in different churches, the only fixed rule being that there should be at least one light on the altar at the time of Mass.[2] Rich churches would have more, and it was the custom to vary the number according to the day or service,[3] but the greater number of parish churches probably had ordinarily only two lights on the high altar, and one on each side altar.[4]

---

[1] The first item in the inventory of goods belonging to the parish of St. Christopher le Stocks, London, in 1488, is "a grete Crosse with Mari and John of silver and over-gilde weyenge iiij^{xx}xj uncis, of the gifte of William Gardyner, draper, and a foote therto of coper and gilt." Further on in the list is entered "a cross-Staffe of coper and gilte that is for the best Crosse that cost the parishoners xviis."

[2] "*Tempore quo missarum solennia peraguntur accendentur due candele vel ad minus una.*" Constitution of Archbishop Walter Raynold, of Canterbury, in 1322. (Lyndewode, *Provinciale*, lib. iii. De celebratione missarum. Lintheamina, fo. clxxj.)

[3] The parish of St. Christopher le Stocks had in 1488 "ij candelstykkes of a sewte to sett on smaller tapers uppon the alters and to bere tapers uppon of laton," and "ij laton candelstykkes with ij noses to set in talowe candell for the alters." In 1862 the walls behind the sites of the two altars at the sides of the chancel arch at Westmeston in Sussex were cleaned of whitewash and amongst remains of painting were found three smoke stains over each altar marking the number and position of the lights formerly used there. This wall is figured in the *Sussex Archæological Collections*, 1864. xvi. plate I. I am indebted to Mr. Leland Duncan for the following very curious extract, as well as for several other passages from unpublished wills which will be used later. This is from the will of Thomas Maldon of Sudbury, Suffolk, mercer (1503): "The Sonday next after my decease a devoute and a goode secular preest shall sey for my soule vij masses that is to sey on the Sonday to begynne w^t the masse of the Trynitie and at the seid masse iiij candells to bren on the seid awter or besid[e] duryng the masse and iij ob. lovys to iiij poore folks in almesse. Also the Monday the masse of ix orders of aungells w^t ix candells brennyng and ix ob. lovys in almesse. Also the Thewsday masse of the iiij Eufigeliste w^t iiij candells brennyng and iiij ob. lovys in almesse. Also the Wednysday the masse of xij apostells w^t xij candells brennyng and xij ob. lovys in almesse. Also on the Thursday the masse of the holy goost w^t vij caundells brennyng and vij ob. lovys in almesse. Also the Friday masse of the crosse w^t v candells brennyng and v ob. lovys in almesse. Also the Satirday the masse of o^r blessid Lady w^t vij candells brennyng and vij ob. lovys in almesse. and those foreseid masses to be said de die in diem w^t. out interrupsion of any other masse." (Somerset House, Prerogative Court of Canterbury, 26 Blamyr.)

[4] "Too standars of Lattyne for the hey alter and too amalle lattyne kandylstyskys for the same." (Inventory of goods in the church of Wing, Bucks, in *Archæologia*, 1855. xxxvi. p. 222, &c.) Myrc in his *Instructions for parish priests* (line 1875. p. 58. edited for the *Early English Text Society* by Mr. E. Peacock) assumes the use of only one light:
"Loke that thy candel of wax hyt be,
And set hyre, so that thow hyre se,
On the lyfte half of thyn autere
And loke algate ho brenne clere."

On occasions the number used might be very great,[1] but as a rule the extra lights were put round about the altar rather than on it. The lights were used at Mattins, Mass, and Evensong. The modern custom of having several sets of candles on an altar at the same time for use at different services has no authority in antiquity.

THE TEXTUS, OR GOSPEL BOOK. The custom of placing a specially ornamented book of the Gospels upon the altar is of very early date. It was kept up in most collegiate churches in 1548, but it seems not to have been usual in the parish churches.

THE ALTAR LECTERN OR CUSHION. The priest's book at the altar was supported, sometimes on a small desk and sometimes on a cushion.[2]

OTHER ORNAMENTS OF THE ALTAR. So long as they remained, reliquaries had been the chief means of decking altars. Figures and other sculptures in alabaster or wood, and especially in the precious metals, were used; and indeed any pieces of plate seem to have been considered proper ornaments for the altar.[3] There is no

---

[1] See the curious particulars of the annual procession to St. Bartholomew's chapel, from the Custom book of the borough of Sandwich (A.D. 1301), printed by Boys in his *History of Sandwich* (p. 87). There were carried in the procession seven score and more of candles (*usque ad numerum vij^{xx} et amplius*) provided at the public cost, besides others found by private persons. When the chapel was reached, the candles were set *super candelabra et alias trabes ad hoc assignatas*. Then followed high Mass. The candles offered on that day were enough to serve the chapel for the whole year following and leave something over, which was returned and worked up again for the next year's offering.

[2] "iij letternes of tre for the iij alters." (St. Christopher le Stocks in 1488.) In 1402 Matilda, wife of John de Smeton of York, left to the high altar of her parish church, "*j cervical, anglice*, a kode, *de panno serico*." (*Test. Ebor.* i. 288.) "*j lettron pro missali.*" (Finchale in 1481. *Transactions of the Architectural and Archæological Society of Durham and Northumberland*, 1593. iv. 137.)

[3] In 1483 Richard the Third went in state to the minster at York, and the high altar was decked with the King's stuff *cum xij Apostolis argenteis et deauratis cum multis aliis reliquiis*. (*York Fabric Rolls*, p. 211.) It is very likely that these images of the apostles were the same that afterwards stood in King Henry's chapel at Guisnes and are recorded by Hall to have been of gold. The word *reliquiis* in this quotation should be noticed. Both *relic* and *jewel* were used in a wide sense for any article, especially one of precious metal, placed upon an altar for its adornment. The metal dishes, which till lately were common upon English altars, but are now going out of fashion, may have a respectable antiquity claimed for them. Witness this extract from the will of Sir W. Bruges in 1449: "Y bequethe to the said church [St. George's Stamford] for ther solempne fest dayes, to stande upon the high awter ij grete basyne of sylver. (See Nichols's *Illustrations of Ancient Manners and Expenses*, p. 132.) Some like examples will be noted when we come to consider alms basons.

evidence of the use of pots or "vases" of flowers.¹ What are now called *altar cards* were unknown in the English Church till they were introduced from abroad a few years ago. But there was a custom to place cards or tablets with the names of persons to be prayed for, and sometimes notes of special prayers to be said, on or near altars at which services for the dead were kept, and where there were endowed services, these sometimes became permanent inscriptions.²

STANDING CANDLESTICKS. In well furnished churches it was usual to have a pair of tall candlesticks of brass or other material placed one on each side in front of the high altar. Sometimes minor altars had them also.³

THE CHALICE. THE PATEN. THE CHALICE SPOON. THE CORPORAS. THE PALLA. THE CORPORAS CASE. Some churches now possess a spoon among their plate. It is, generally, a domestic spoon, which has been given by someone for the use of the altar. The same used to be done in the middle ages, but sometimes the spoons were purposely made.⁴ The corporas case or forel was used to keep the folded

---

[1] Although flowers were not used to deck altars, garlands of them were sometimes worn by the clergy and others, and now and then a reference to this custom is found in church accounts. At St. Stephen's Walbrook in 1525, a penny was "paid for a garland of Rosays apon chyrche hallyday," that is upon the dedication feast. And again the next year for *Corpus Christi* day threepence was "payd for garlondes." These last were perhaps for those who bore the canopy. Such garlands had sometimes been used to crown images, especially those of the patron Saints of churches, and we find artificial flowers so used at St. Stephen's about 1481, "a garlonde of flowris for his [that is St. Stephen's] hed of wyre and silke of the parson's yifte."

[2] Such a one in the form of a brass plate still remains affixed to the wall near the lavatory in the chancel of Morley Church, Derbyshire. In 1405 Richard Wartroe of York, after giving directions in his will for services to be said for him and others after his death, directs that his executors shall write or cause to be written "*sedulas seu billas*" with the testator's name and those of his near relations "*ita ut omnes predicti capellani mei qui pro anima mea concelebrabunt habeant seu habeat unus-quisque eorundum unam billam ad altaria sua, ea intencione ut habeant me in memoria et specialiter et devote orent.*" (*Test. Ebor.* ii. 274.)

[3] It appears from various accounts quoted in Kerry's *History of the Church of St. Laurence, Reading*, that three side altars in that church had standing candlesticks of brass before them. "ij greatt standards" in the Lady chapel are mentioned in 1524 (p. 36) "a payre of greto candylstykkes" at the altar of St. John Baptist bought in 1505 weighed 103 lbs. (p. 37) and "ij grete standards of latten" in St. Thomas's chapel also mentioned in 1524 (p. 41). There was a pair at the high altar besides these.

[4] See will of John Ravensthorpe of York, 1432, "*calicem sanctifica:um cum patena et cocliari eidem calici pertinentes.*" (*Test. Ebor.* ii. 29.) Also given to York Minster in 1370, "*unum coclear argenti deauratum ad proporcionandum vinum sive aquam pro calice magni altaris.*" (*York Fabric Rolls*, p. 185.)

corporas in. The *palla* is seldom mentioned as a separate ornament, as it was really another corporas, one cloth being opened out and laid upon the altar, and the other kept folded to cover the chalice with.[1] The square of pasteboard cased in linen which has been introduced from abroad into a few of our churches lately and is called a pall, has no English authority, and the use of pasteboard or paper in the place of linen about the Blessed Sacrament is contrary to some of the oldest canons.

THE STANDING PYX. Lists of church goods often include a *cup* to hold the Sacrament. Sometimes, especially where it is described to be of inferior metal, it was probably the hanging vessel in which the pyx was placed for suspension, but in other cases it may have been for use at Communion time when the number of communicants was large. There is preserved in the church of Wymeswold, Leicestershire, a silver vessel which is believed by some to have been for this use.[2] The name *Standing pyx* describes it well, but it is also used for a monstrance and for a reliquary in the form of a monstrance. The inventories do not always make it clear for what use an ornament so entered is intended.

THE CREWETS FOR WINE AND WATER. They were generally of silver or pewter; and the difference between them was marked in various ways, as by one being gilt and the other plain, or by letters or other ornaments.[3]

A BOX FOR ALTAR BREADS. Rich churches had these of silver.[4]

THE SUDARY was a scarf of silk or linen which was cast

---

[1] Early inventories and the like often mention the corporases in pairs, as "*viij paria corporalium cum forellis v.*" in the Sarum inventory of 1222, printed by Dr. Rock at the end of his *Church of our Fathers*: and "*deficit unum par Corporalium,*" from a visitation of the Church of Bosham in 1282, in Mr. Hingeston-Randolph's *Register* of Bishop Quivil of Exeter, p. 316. The later inventory-makers seem to have concerned themselves chiefly with the cases, which were more costly things than the corporases, which they sometimes do not even mention. The following entry in an inventory of All Souls' College Oxford in 1488 seems to shew that both cloths were kept in one case. "*j tecam cum armis Domini gemmis textam cum duobus corporalibus in eadem.*"

[2] It bears the London hall mark for 1512-3 and the cover, if ever there were one, is lost. This vessel is figured in the *Proceedings of the Society of Antiquaries*, 1886. xi. 59.

[3] "*viij crowettes de electro. ij crewettes argenteae unde j deaurata*" (Finchale, 1481.)

[4] "*una pixis argenti cum scriptura circa eandem* Elige de optimis *pro pane portando diebus ferialibus. pond. z unc. di.*" (Inventory of goods at York Minster in 1510. *York Fabric Rolls*, p. 221.)

about the shoulders and in the ends of which the hands of those who carried certain objects ceremonially were muffled. In quires it was used by the patener or third minister when he brought in the chalice and when he held up the paten. But in parish churches its chief use was to carry the chrismatory at the solemn processions to the font at Eastertide. When not of linen it seems to have usually been made of some old stuff of little worth.[1] There is some resemblance between the sudary and the modern silken chalice veil, which may be a remnant of it.

THE CENSER. THE SHIP. THE SPOON FOR INCENSE. The censer was amongst the things which were to be found by the parishioners, and few churches seem to have been without it.

TWO BASONS FOR WASHING THE HANDS. A TOWEL. The usual English custom seems to have been to use, not a ewer and bason, but two basons for the washing of the hands of the celebrant. Water was poured from one to the other, and sometimes one had a spout at the side for the purpose.[2] The towel sometimes hung on the wall at the south side of the presbytery.[3]

THE SUPERALTAR. This was a small portable consecrated altar stone intended to be placed upon a table when there was a celebration in an unconsecrated place, or to be used when a consecrated altar was wanting. The privilege of private services was granted to a man personally, and only to a few. It is likely that some of the superaltars which were possessed by parish churches,[4] had been bequeathed

[1] "An olde Clothe of Silk for berin the Crysmatorye to the Ffounte." (From an inventory of Great St. Mary's Church, Cambridge, in 1504, quoted in Sandars's *Historical and Architectural Notes* on that church, p. 49.) "A Sewdarie of grene tarterne ffringed with silke on both ends." (St. Christopher le Stocks 1488.) "A sudary of red sarcynett conteynynge in leynth ij. yardes di: and in brede a quarter di:." (Boston in 1534, see Peacock's *Church Furniture*, p. 204.)

[2] Amongst divers things given to York Minster in 1370 we find "*duas pelves argenti deauratas bene spissas cum armis Angliae et Franciae in fundis bipartitis, quarum una habet bibonam.*" (*York Fabric Rolls*, p. 185.) At St. Mary's, Scarborough, they had in 1484 "*duæ pelves argenti pro Lavatorio*" (p. 67.) and "*quinque manutergia pro lavatorio*" (p. 66).

[3] At Bishop's Stortford in 1548 they had "a trendyll for a towell ayenst the awter end," which I understand as a roller for a jack towel. (See Glasscock, *Records of St. Michael's Parish Church, Bishop's Stortford*, 1882. p. 131.)

[4] The Church of St. Christopher le Stocks had three in 1488. In the first year of Queen Mary the authorities of Gray's Inn set up a wooden altar in their chapel, and amongst the charges about it is entered "a Super Altare 1s. 8d." and "104. foot of Oaken board for the Altar." (Douthwaite's *Gray's Inn*, Lond. 1886. p. 147.) We may

to them by those who had in their lives had the privilege. They had no use in a church which had its own consecrated altars, and were probably only looked upon as "jewels" for the decking of the altars at feasts.

REGISTERS. Sometimes a register is mentioned amongst the plate belonging to a church. It was a book marker in the form of a thin strip of silver with ornamental ends.[1]

THE SACKERING BELL. The ringing of bells during the time of service had been forbidden by the injunctions, except before the sermon, and if any bell were rung then it would be one of the bells in the steeple audible to people outside. Some use of the small bell inside the church seems, however, to have continued even till the total stopping of the church services during the puritan usurpation in the seventeenth century. The bells were generally handbells, but sometimes were hung against walls or on screens. Sometimes they were in sets to sound together; and in one case, which probably was not singular at the time, we find the sackering bell developed into a musical chime.[2]

PROCESSIONAL CROSS. PROCESSIONAL CANDLESTICKS AND TORCHES. These must have continued in use so far, at least, as they belonged to the service at the altar as long as the *Order of Communion* was in force. Torches are not mentioned in the rubrics, but they appear so often in pictured or sculptured representations of the Mass[3] as

---

infer from this that the earlier wooden altars, already referred to, were furnished with superaltars when used. At All Saints Derby there was in 1466 "a super Altare that Thoms Sharpuls gaffe." (J. C. Cox and W. H. St. John Hope, *The Chronicles . . . of All Saints, Derby*, Lond. 1881. p. 160.)

[1] St. Mary's Guild in Boston had in 1534 "a register of silver longynge to a portas with an acorne of ether ende" (Peacock, p. 208.)

[2] The will of John Baret, of Bury (1463), which contains much that illustrates the condition of a good town church in the fifteenth century, mentions this, and further directs that the "berere of the paxbrede" should "wynde up the plumme of led as ofte as nedith" and "do the chymes goo at ye sacry of the Messe." (*Bury Wills*, p. 29.) High up against the west wall of the south transept of Milton Abbey

church, Dorset, there is fixed a tall turret of open woodwork. By the help of the vicar, the Rev. E. H. Bousfield, I was lately able to get up to it and examine it closely. There are remains of clockwork inside and I have little doubt that it is the case for a set of chimes such as existed at Bury. There is a like turret against the north wall of the presbytery in the abbey church of Tewkesbury.

[3] For example, on those fonts in Norfolk and Suffolk which have upon them representations of the seven sacraments. It may be noted that the torch is most often shown of a green colour. In 1400, John Preston, of York, left money "*ad sustentacionem duorum torcheorum cotidie ad elevacionem sacro sanctae Hostiae illuminandorum.*" (*Test. Ebor.* i. 269.) In 1481 the "Worshipfull" of the parish of St. Nicholas, Bristol, made an agreement

THE ORNAMENTS OF THE RUBRIC. 37

to leave no doubt that it was the common custom to light one or more at the consecration, or *sackering*, as it was called. There was usually a special cross for Lent, often of wood, painted red, or sometimes green, and generally without any figure.[1] At Easter they used, in most places, to hang a banner to the cross, and it was often done at other feasts.[2] These banners had devices suited to the time, as the Resurrection, or the picture of the patron saint.[3] Sometimes a tall locker or closet was formed in the wall of a church to keep the processional cross in. It is found in different positions but oftenest either near the high altar or near the principal door. There is an example of the former at St. Mary's Church Sandwich, and one of the latter at St. Sepulchre's Church Northampton.

THE MONSTRANCE, OR OOSTER. Nothing like the modern Roman office of Benediction ever existed in the Church of England, but the monstrance was used when the Sacrament was carried solemnly in procession, which was done on Palm Sunday, Easter Day, and Corpus Christi day, and occasionally at other times. It was made in various forms.[4] One, which seems to have been specially used for the procession on Easter morning, was an image of our Lord with a pyx of crystal or glass

---

recorded in a paper entitled "Howe the Clerke and the Suffrigan of Seynt Nicholas Church ought to do." It has been edited by Colonel Bramble, F.S.A., and printed by the Clifton Antiquarian Club, being No. III of the series of *Ancient Bristol documents*, p. 143. It is therein ordered that "The undirsofregan . . . shall se that ij Torches on the Sondaye be brennyng at the hygh masse sacryng" and again "The suffrygan to se that there be a torche redy for the messes that is sayde in the churche dayly." *Suffrigan* would seem to be a corruption of *Sacristan*.

[1] At St. Margaret Pattens, London, in 1486, they had "a crosse and a Crosse staffe to serve for lentton, payntid green withoute ymages wt iij white silver nailis." (Inventory in *Archæological Journal*, xlii. 322.)

[2] Clement Maydeston in his tract *Crede Michi* (*Tracts of Clement Maydestone*, ed. by Chr. Wordsworth, Henry Bradshaw Society, 1894. p. 53.) says: "*In Ecclesia Sarum. et secundum ordinale Sarum. nunquam portatur crux cum vexillo. sicut habetur in multis ecclesijs.*" But the practice must have been very common amongst churches which followed the Sarum use. Some York Mass books have a rubric directing the procession on Easter Even to go "*cruce nudata et vexillo in cruce appenso.*"

[3] Item ij crosse banners of grene silke that on of theym beten wt the resurreccion And the tother of theym beten wt the ymage of Seynt Margarett," and again "Itm a crosse cloth steyned wt the resurreccion." (p. 319. Inventory of St. Margaret Pattens, 1470.) "A cross of laten with Mary and John with a staff and a banner of sarenete of the Salutation," returned by Churchwardens as belonging to the church of Barnes in 1552. (Tyssen, *Surrey Inventories*, p. 90.)

[4] Great St. Mary's Church, Cambridge, had "a Sonne of Silver and gilte for the Sacrament." It was small and weighed only three ounces and a quarter. (Sandars's *Historical and Architectural Notes*, p. 54.)

fixed to the breast.[1] It was usual in towns where there were several churches for them to join in one procession on Corpus Christi day, and when this was done the monstrance was sometimes fixed in a large shrine made for the purpose and carried by two or four men.[2]

THE PAX. THE HOLY WATER VAT AND SPRINKLE. THE SKEP FOR HOLY BREAD. I have put these together because of the curious evidence of the retention of all of them at this time, which we have in the injunctions of a commission of magistrates, who were directed to visit the churches of the Deanery of Doncaster, in 1548, to see that the various changes which had been ordered up to that time were properly carried out. Their injunctions are printed in Wilkins's *Concilia*,[3] and I know of no other like document, but it is probable that similar commissions may have been issued in other places. The commissioners gave various instructions as to the manner of performing the service, including directions for the sprinkling with holy water before the service, the presentation of the pax to the people by the clerk, and the distribution of the holy bread.[4]

---

[1] Lincoln cathedral church in 1548 had "an Image of our Saviour silver and guilt standing uppon 6 Lions void in y⁵ brest for y⁶ Sacrament for Easter day, haveing a bearll before, and a Diademe behind wth a Crosse in hand, weighing xxxvij unces" (p. 45.) In 1466 the parish of St. Stephen Coleman Street London amongst its "Juelis" had "the resurrecion of our lorde w^t the avyse in hys bosum to put the sacrament therin." (p. 34.) It also had "a mone of sylver to ber the sacrament." (p. 34.) and "a monstrance of sylver for the sacrament w^t the bande of oure lady in the vise above the by auter." (p. 34.) At Westminster abbey at the suppression there was "a Nooster for the Sacrament of curius work of sylver and gylt haveing a berall in it cxliiij unces." (p. 317.)

[2] See the description of that used at Durham in the *Rites of Durham Abbey* (Surtees Soc. edition), p. 90. That at Lincoln minster in 1548 was a costly thing. It is thus described in the inventory: "one great Fertur silver and guilt wth one Crosse Iles and one Stepell in y Middle and one Crosse in y⁶ toppe wth twentye Pinnacles and an Image of our Lady in one end and an Image of St. Hugh in y⁶ other end haveing in length half a yard and one ynche, and it is sett in a Table of Wood, and athing in y⁶ middle to put in y⁶ Sacrament when it is borne weighing $\left\{ \begin{array}{c} 1^{xx} \ldots vij \\ 340 \end{array} \right\}$ unces and one wanting a Pinnacle." (p. 44.) This had been given to the church by John Welborne its treasurer who died in 1381.

[3] Lond. 1737. iv. 29. There are some evident mistakes in the transcript.

[4] The *holy loaf* which provided the holy bread used to be found by the principal householders of a parish in turn, and it was offered each Sunday, generally with a candle and a piece of money, either at the beginning of the Mass or at the offertory. In the book of 1549 an attempt was made to retain this offering but to divert it to a new use. The rubrics at the end of the Mass in that book direct that on each Sunday, the parishioners should offer at the time of the offertory "the just valour of the holy loaf with all such money and other things as were wont to be offered with the same to the use of the pastors and curates, and that in such order as they were wont to find and pay the said holy loaf." It was also ordered that "Some

THE HOUSELING CLOTH. A long linen cloth held by clerks in front of the communicants when receiving the Sacrament, or sometimes laid upon a bench at which they knelt. In some cases it seems to have been long enough to reach all across the nave and aisles of the church.[1] In a manner it took the place of the altar rail of modern times, though Communion was not necessarily given at an altar. The rail was not used at the date of our inquiry: it was introduced early in the next century. The houseling cloth was ordinarily of linen, but on state occasions it was sometimes of silk.[2] Its use continued long after the reformation and is even yet not quite extinct.

ALMS BASONS. The inventory of goods of the Church of St. Christopher le Stocks, in 1488, has "ij coper Disshes to gedre offryng inne," and that of St. Margaret Pattens in 1470 has "an Offeryng dissh of Coper." The silver basons, the use of which as altar ornaments has been mentioned, were also used to receive offerings as appears from the will quoted in the note below.[3] From their weight the "ij Basons of Silver with Leggys Armes,

one at least of the house in every parish to whom by course, after the ordinance herein made, it appertaineth to offer for the charges of the Communion, or some other whom they shall provide to offer for them, shall receive the Holy Communion with the priest." Up to this date, though solitary Masses had been forbidden, the want of Communicants did not prevent the celebration of the Sunday Mass, but this attempt was made to ensure that they should not be wanting.

[1] I have found mention of these cloths as much as twenty yards long. I select the following quotation for the sake of the name *mensa Domini*, which is evidently given not to the altar but to the bench or desk against which the communicants knelt, and upon which the houseling cloth was laid: "*Unum manutergium continens undecim ulnas ecclesiae meas parochiali, ut possit servire ad mensam Domini in die Paschae.*" Will of Agnes de Selby in 1359. (*Test. Ebor.* i. 71.) So too Joan Goodewyn, widow, in 1515, left to the parish church of Bromley in Kent "a tuell to be forth comyng at Eastre, whan our blessid lorde is mynistrid unto the parisch." (Somerset House, Rochester Wills, vii. fol. 145. I owe this instance again to Mr. Leland L. Duncan.)

[2] In the *Device for the coronation of King Henry VII.* (*Rutland Papers,* Camden Society, 1842. p. 22.) "ij [of] the grettest astate then present holding befor the King and the Quene a long towell of silke." This was only for ostentation. Other things, properly of linen, were sometimes made of silk. Albes and surplices of silk will be noted further on. The very early canons which forbid the use of silk in the place of linen on the altar, prove, that from a misdirected desire to do honour to the Sacrament, the change must sometimes have been made.

[3] "I geve to the parisshe church of Seynt Mary Wolnoth two of my basons of silver parcell gilt weyeng cxxij unces di: in the botom wherof the holy name of Ihū is graven to thentent that the same basons to the lawde praysing and honor of Almighty God shall serve and be sett forth upon the high awter ther in tymes and fests there convenyent for evermore, and to be occupied at such tymes and fests convenyent for to receyve in theym the offerings there to be made." (Will of Sir John Percyvale, knight, and late Mayor of London, 1502, Somerset House, Prerogative Court of Canterbury, 23 Blamyr.) I owe this reference to Mr. Leland L. Duncan.

weyeng lix ownces" which also belonged to St. Christopher's le Stocks seem more likely to have been what we should now call alms dishes than basons for the lavatory.

THE LECTERN FOR THE GOSPEL. Richly furnished churches had often brass desks standing on the north side of the presbytery to sing the Gospel from. The eagle desks which remain in some old parish churches,[1] and are now generally used to hold the great Bible, were, in most cases, originally meant for the Gospel. In a few churches, chiefly in Derbyshire, stone gospel desks are found against the north wall. Such exist at Mickleover, at Crich, and at Chaddesden, all in Derbyshire. Before the changes of the sixteenth century began the gospel and epistle were read in parish churches either at the altar or near to it. But for some time before 1548 these lessons had been read in English, and it was ordered to be done either in the pulpit or in such a place that the people might conveniently hear them, and it seems that in some churches a platform was made for this use in the body of the church.[2] Good examples of brass desks for the Gospel remain at Oundle, Northamptonshire; Long Sutton, Lincolnshire; and St. Margaret's, King's Lynn.[3]

THE LAVATORY. Near the south end of each altar was a small lavatory, called in Latin *sacrarium* or *piscina*, and above or near it was a shelf or bracket upon which the crewets were placed. The credence, in the form of a table, seems not to have been used here before the seventeenth century. The old English custom at plain services, and at most services in parish churches, seems to have been to place the chalice at the south end of the altar at the beginning of the service, and to take it thence to the middle of the altar at the time of offering, thus making the end of the altar itself serve as a credence. At solemn services *cum tribus ministris* in quires, the chalice was

---

[1] Most of those in cathedral churches are of the seventeenth century.

[2] In 1547, the churchwardens of St. Margaret's, Westminster, paid two shillings "for making of the stone in the body of the church, for the priest to declare the Pistells and Gospells"; and in 1553, thirteen shillings and fourpence for "the pulpit, where the Curate and the Clark did read the chapters at service-time." (Nichols's *Illustrations*, pp. 12 and 14.)

[3] Dame Maud Spicer who died in 1498 gave to All Saints, Bristol, an eagle of laten for the gospel to be read upon, price £viii. (Nicholls, J. F. and Taylor, John, *Bristol past and present*, Bristol, Arrowsmith, 1881. ii. 96.)

"made" at a side altar, or other fit place some distance away, so that by the stateliness of the approach greater dignity might be given to the ceremonial offering. Until the suppression of the monasteries, the more ascetic orders, the Cistercians, Carthusians, and White Canons, who had a simpler ceremonial than that followed in the great secular churches, did use the credence, which they called *ministerium*.[1]

THE SEDILIA. This is a modern name for the seats of the clergy at the south side of the presbytery.[2] They varied in number but were seldom more than three, except in great "quires," where they were generally four.

We have now been through the list of the ornaments of the church, so far as they belong to the service at the altar. Next we will take those of the quire. As to these there was much difference amongst churches, according to the style of service which was kept up in them, from the stately minster, with its many clergy and its endowed singers, to the humble moorland church, served occasionally by a priest and clerk only. The collegiate churches had their full sung services every day; and with the prosperity of the middle classes in the fourteenth and fifteenth centuries there had grown up a desire to improve the services of the parish churches, in which they worshipped, until, at the time of our enquiry, some of those in towns were not far behind the colleges. One consequence of this was the introduction into the parish

---

[1] Sometimes a stone with a sunk and pierced bowl like that of a piscina is found in the floor near the south end of an altar. These floor sinks have been supposed to be a variety of the piscina, but evidently they are not that, for the piscina of the ordinary form is generally found in the wall near to them. Durandus (*Rat. Div. Off.* lib. IV. cap. xxx. § 20.) tells us that in his time it was the custom to pour out a few drops from the crewets to clear the spouts of dust before "making" the chalice, and it is most likely that these sinks were intended to receive what was so poured out. I doubt whether they were in use at the time we are studying, for such examples as can be dated are much older than that. The frequent disturbance of floors has not left many of them in parish churches; but there is one at Little Casterton in Rutland. Lincoln and Gloucester cathedrals have examples, and they are common amongst the Cistercian ruins in Yorkshire.

[2] What we call the sedilia is the last remnant of the bench which in primitive times ran all round the apse and was assigned to the priests; whence probably by tradition came the name *presbytery* which seems to have been their old English name. ("j cloth of grene bokrume lyned for the presbetory," St. Stephen's Coleman Street, 1466, p. 42.) In the contract for the rebuilding of Catterick church (1412.) they are called *three prismatories*, an evident corruption or miswriting of *presbyteries*. (James Raine, *Catterick Church . . . contract for its building*, Lond. J. Weale, 1834. p. 9.)

chancel of various things which originally belonged to the collegiate "quire." But tradition ruled less in the parish churches than in the quires, and the services in them were, to use a modern word, of a more "popular" character.

SCREENS. The chancel, as the name (*cancellus*) implies, was separated from the rest of the church by screens, and the same was done for each chapel and altar.

THE ROOD LOFT. It was usual in parish churches, even in the smallest, to have a gallery on the top of the screen which separated the chancel from the nave. This is one of the adaptations from the quire. , It is not the same as the *pulpitum* of a quire, but it was suggested by it, and served some of the same uses. It was a music gallery. It was not used for the gospel and epistle, but certain parts of the services were sung there, and it was occupied by the "minstrels," whom it was the custom for well-to-do parishes to hire to sing the service on high days. These minstrels sang pricksong, accompanied by instruments of various sorts.

OTHER LOFTS. Occasionally small lofts are found in other positions, as over the screens of chapels, and sometimes above the arch leading to a west tower; these were probably also music galleries. The gallery inside a west tower was for the convenience of ringers.

THE ROOD. From very early times it had been the custom to set up a large cross in the midst of a church, and in England it was placed over the entrance to the chancel, either upon the screen itself, or upon the wall or a beam above it. I can not find anything which gives the "authority of Parliament" for the destruction of the roods in 1548, though it was being done in places by certain called the "King's Majesty's Commissioners." In Elizabeth's time, when the standard of the second year of Edward VI. was chosen to fix the new use as to church ornaments, the rood was not reckoned amongst the superstitious images, which were to be abolished. The Queen was herself anxious to keep it, and did so for a time; but afterwards the efforts of the foreign-bred Puritans amongst the bishops prevailed to its destruction, The rood always had a figure of our Lord crucified. and generally images of St. Mary and St. John at the

THE ORNAMENTS OF THE RUBRIC.   43

sides. In rich churches other figures were added, those of angels being the most usual.[1]

STALLS AND DESKS. Well furnished churches had stalls with *misericords*, or turn-up seats, and desks on each side of the chancel, and returned at the west against the screen. Parish churches had only one row of stalls, but sometimes there was a bench in front of the desks for the use of the song boys. Poor churches had plain settles instead of stalls. In large collegiate churches, where service was regularly sung in the Lady chapels, they were sometimes fitted up like quires; but this was never done in the Lady chapel of an ordinary parish church.

THE GREAT LECTERN. In the middle of the chancel stood a lectern of wood or brass, generally of two desks made to turn. On it lay the grayle and the antiphoner, the music books belonging, respectively, to the services of the altar and the quire.

LECTERN CLOTH. Amongst the ornaments is sometimes mentioned a cloth for the lectern. It was a long strip, which went over the desk of the lectern, and hung below it before and behind.

LESSER LECTERNS. Mention is sometimes made of small lecterns standing in the quire and the rood loft.[2] They were what we should now call music stands.

THE ORGAN. A well appointed church generally had an organ. It was small, and usually stood in the rood loft.[3]

CHANTERS' STOOLS. CHANTERS' STAVES. In imitation of the quires, some parish churches used to have chanters or

---

[1] "To the makyng and peyntyng of a new crucifix upon the candelbome with Mary and John & Archangelys aftir Dedham" (will of John Beylham in 1500, Reg. F. Canterbury, folio 37ª). Here *candelbeme* means the rood loft for which it was the usual name in the eastern counties. *After Dedham* means after the fashion of those then already existing at Dedham. It was in the rood loft, and not on the altar as in some modern churches, that lights were extravagantly multiplied. St. Stephen's Coleman Street in 1466 had "xxvij" disshes for the beme lyghte in the rode lofte." This is "the light that commonly goeth across the church by the rood loft," which was specially retained in Cromwell's *Injunctions* in 1536, when most others were forbidden. And it sufficiently explains the name *candlebeam*. The exception was not repeated in the *Injunctions* of 1547, so the beam light must be taken as forbidden by such authority as they had.

[2] In 1488 St. Christopher's le Stocks had an iron standing lectern and two wooden ones in the rood loft, and two in the quire, besides the "grete deske lettarne for the gret Boke." (p. 119.)

[3] "Also in the same Rode lofte is a peyre Orgons and a lyd over the keys wᵗ lok and keye." "Also, a stondyng lecterne fer to ley on a boke to pleyu by." "Also a stolo to sit on when he pleythe on the Orgons." (St. Stephen's Walbrook, c. 1480, p. 342.)

rulers of the quire, or, as they often called them, *standers*.[1] Copes[2] and stools[3] for them are mentioned occasionally, but I do not remember to have met with chanters' staves in any inventory of parish goods. They probably used plain wands which were of small value, and so not worth recording.

THE ROWELL. THE TRENDLE. In churchwardens' accounts we sometimes meet with an entry like " p^d. for a Rope to the Rowyll "[4] " for a bolte and a swevyll to the trendyll "[5] or for wax for one or the other. The Rowell and the Trendle were I think the same thing. It seems to have belonged to Christmastide and to have been in use in many places, but not to have had any special ceremony connected with it as the paschal candle had. It should perhaps be regarded more as a piece of decoration, such as the wreaths and banners which people put up now, than an ecclesiastical ornament. Each word means a wheel, and the thing itself seems to have been a hoop with candles fixed to it which was hung up in the chancel from Christmas to Candlemas, and was intended to represent the star of the Wise men.[6]

POOR MAN'S BOX. The injunctions of 1547 order the provision of a chest with three keys near the high altar. Till the " restorers " took them away, such chests remained in some places on one side of the chancel, just below the step of the presbytery. Collecting boxes of earlier date are sometimes found. They had been common in connexion with shrines and images so long as such remained.

PEWS. Most churches had pews for the use of the

---

[1] " Four copes of crimson velvet, plaine, with orphreys of clothe of goulde, for standers." (*York Fabric Rolls*, p. 309.)

[2] In 1530 William Leryffax, of Beverley, left by will a house to be sold, and the proceeds to be spent in a full suit of vestments for St. Mary's Church there, including "two copies to stand in the qwhere" or four "yff the money will mount so fer." (*Test. Ebor.* v. 209.)

[3] " For two stolys [stools] for the rectors of the quyre." (*Churchwardens' accounts* for St. Mary's-at-Hill, London, 1531, printed in Nichols's *Illustrations*, p. 109.)

[4] Accounts of St. Michael's, Spurrier gate, York, in Nichols's *Illustrations*, p. 313.

[5] At Reading, Kerry, p. 53.

[6] At St. Lawrence's, Reading, in 1506, they "payed for sysis to the holy bush at Christmas ix^d," and "for an holy bush before the Rode ij^d. (Kerry, p. 52.) Thus they put before the rood a holly bush with syses or small tapers in it. The resemblance of this to the modern Christmas tree introduced amongst us quite lately from Germany is curious, but a connexion between them is not likely. The bush was probably the whim of some decorator. There seems to have been such a one about, for we also read that they set up a frame with angels holding candles.

people, though they were not crowded with them as became the custom at a later date. They generally occupied only the eastern part of the nave and of the aisles (where there were any) the passages between the blocks being very wide. When a church had chapels at the sides of the chancel they also were often fitted with pews, arranged so that they might be used by worshippers either at the high altar or at the altars of the respective chapels. Shut up pews or *closets*, as they were called, were to be found in some churches. They were generally the enclosures about altars at which there had been chantries, and were used by the patrons of the chantries as private pews. This use continued after the suppression of the chantries.

PULPIT. This was ordered by the injunctions of 1547 to be provided where it did not already exist.

A DESK FOR BOOKS. The great Bible was to be placed where the people might have access to it, and the *Paraphrases* of Erasmus were also to be provided for the reading of the people. This would need a reading desk of some sort. The custom of placing books of devotion or instruction in the church for the private reading of the people had been used before this,[1] and it became very common in the seventeenth century.

TABLES WITH INSCRIPTIONS. Besides books there were placed in many churches framed tablets with writings for the instruction and edification of the people. As early as 1488, we find the ten commandments set up at St. Christopher's le Stocks, with "dyuerse good prayers."[2] And instead of the hymn book of our time the church of St. Stephen Coleman Street had in 1466 "j salve tabyll Couered wt a lynnen clothe Item j nothir of the tunery."[3] "Item j of the antymys of the cros and oure lady and the responnys of the triuite"[4] and others besides.

THE FONT. THE FONT COVER. THE FONT CLOTH. The

---

[1] There was in 1488 a collection of books in the Vestry of St. Christopher le Stocks for the reading of the clergy and perhaps of others; "on the south side of the vestrarie standeth a grete library with ij longe lecturnalles theron to ley on the bokes." (p. 120.) This "library" was evidently a double faced book case to which books were chained and with a reading desk on each side, such as remain at Merton College Oxford, Hereford Cathedral, and elsewhere. I think this use of the word has not been observed before.

[2] St. Christopher le Stocks, p. 119.
[3] St. Stephen Coleman Street, p. 44.
[4] *idem*, p. 45.

font usually stood near the west end of the nave. The placing of it in a secluded corner called a baptistery is foreign and of very recent introduction amongst us. The so-called baptisteries at Trunch and Luton are not such, but canopies to the fonts, which in both cases stand in the usual place.[1] The cover was kept locked down, as the custom was to keep the font filled with water which was hallowed only occasionally, and not at each baptism as now. The font cloth is an ornament often mentioned in inventories, but I do not remember to have found any reference to it except in them or in churchwardens' accounts, and I am not sure what it was. It was generally of linen, but sometimes of silk.

THE CHRISMATORY. THE SALT. A CANDLE. A EWER AND BASON. A NAPKIN. All these things were used in the old office of baptism, and often a locker was provided near the font to keep them in.[2] The ewer and bason were for the sponsors to wash their hands after taking the child from the font.[3] There is no evidence of the use of a shell or anything of that sort for the affusion of water by the priest. A silver shell is sometimes mentioned amongst church goods. It was most likely used to hold salt in the preparation of holy water,[4] and perhaps also at

---

[1] The octagonal building to the north of the cathedral church at Canterbury, often called a baptistery, was built for a conduit house in connexion with the water supply of the monastery. The font which was put there in comparatively recent times has lately been moved back to its proper place in the church.

[2] The most perfect font locker I have seen was destroyed when the fine old church of Tadcaster was pulled down in 1875. It was in the south-west corner of the north aisle and had some remains of the woodwork and ironwork about the shutter. A locker on the same position still remains at Burford, Oxfordshire. There is one in the north wall of the north aisle at Tilbrook, Bedfordshire, and a double one in the north wall of the west tower at Walpole St. Andrew's, Norfolk. The name *chrismatory* seems to have been given to the locker sometimes as at Leverton in 1541 when they paid "for on lock ij bandes and ij howkes [hooks] for the chrysmatorye viij.d." and "for makyng of the chryssmatorye dore xiiij.d."

[3] In 1466 William Holme, vicar of Mattersey, Notts, left a ewer and bason to his church, adding in his will "*et volo quod hujusmodi pelvis et lavacrum deserviant temporibus baptizacionis infancium.*" (*Test. Ebor.* ii. 279.) A like bequest was made by Agas Herte to the church of St. James, Bury St. Edmunds, in 1522. (See her will printed in *Bury Wills and Inventories*, p. 116.) At Wiggenhale St. Peter, in Norfolk, is a piscina like that of an altar, but in the south wall of the nave, four feet from the west wall. (*Archæological Journal*, 1889. xlvi. 394.) I believe this was for pouring away the water after this washing.

[4] At St. Stephen's chapel, Westminster, where there would be no font, there was at the suppression "a scalope shell of sylver and gylt of xiij. ons:." (*Transactions of London and Middlesex Archæological Society*, 1875. iv. 878.)

baptisms. But churches which could afford silver would generally have different vessels for the two uses.

THE CHRYSOM CLOTH. This was a linen kerchief placed on the head of the infant after the unction which used to follow baptism. It might not be turned again to common use, and was to be brought back to the church. The general custom was for the mother to bring and offer it at her churching, whence the name *shriving cloth* sometimes given to it. The chrysom cloths were made into articles for church use, such as altar cloths and surplices.[1]

THE CHURCHING CLOTH. This was a cloth used at the churching of women. The first extract in the note seems to shew that it was laid over the stool or desk at which they knelt. It seems to have been made of any decent stuff which happened to be available.[2]

HOLY WATER STOCKS. A holy water stock was placed at each of the principal doors of entrance. It was either a stone bason or a vessel of metal, earthenware, or wood placed on a bracket or hung on a pin.

THE SHRIVING PEW. This was what is now called a confessional. It seems to have been common in London, and existed in other places, but I do not think it was in general use. It is sometimes called the *shriving house* and the *shriving stool*. We do not know anything of its form beyond what is suggested by the names. *Irons* are mentioned in connexion with it, and they may have been rods for curtains, and sometimes curtains are named.[3]

---

[1] "Item: an altar cloth made of shryvynge clothes." (Inventory of goods belonging to St. Mary's Guild at Boston. Peacock's *Church Furniture*, p. 204.)

[2] Alice Joye of Hoo, widow, wills in 1513 that "a clothe be bougthe for to laye before women whan they be purified wt a picture of the Purificacion of our ladie the price v{s}." (Somerset House, *Rochester Wills*, Book vii. fol. 15{o}.) In 1604 Great St. Mary's Church, Cambridge, had "a Clothe of Tapestry Werke for chirchyng of Wifs lyned wt Canvas," as appears by an inventory quoted in Sandars's *Historical and Architectural Notes* on the church, p. 49. Wandsworth church in 1552 had "a clothe serving for the purification of silk." (Tyssen's *Surrey Inventories*, pp. 46 and 181.) St. Dunstan's, Canterbury, in 1500 had a "clothe staynyd for the puryficacion off women." (*Archaeologia Cantiana*, 1886. xvi. 314.)

[3] At Great St. Mary's, Cambridge, in 1504, "vj yernes portoyning to the Shryvyng Stole for Lenton." (Sandars's *Notes*, p. 48.) And at Bishop's Stortford in 1525 they paid "for peyntyng of the cloth at the scryvng (*sic*) howse." (Glasscock, *Records of St. Michael's Parish Church, Bishop's Stortford*, p. 39.) Imaginative sextons and such folk are apt to call anything in an old church, which they can not understand, a *confessional*, especially if it has a hole of any sort in it. But I do not think a real one exists. It is possible that the curious chamber at Tanfield, near Ripon, is a confessional; but it seems rather to be a watching closet. It may, perhaps, have served both purposes.

[THE LITANY DESK. This has been so often included in lists purporting to be of the ornaments of the second year of Edward VI. that it is mentioned here, lest it should be thought that it has been inadvertently omitted, but I can not find any evidence of its use so early. The injunctions of 1547 ordered that immediately before High Mass the priest and others of the quire, not the priest alone as is now the custom, should kneel in the midst of the church, and there sing or say, plainly and distinctly, the litany. This was a modification of the old procession, and the litany itself was often called the *Procession*. Some such convenience as the desk very likely soon came into use, but the only mention of anything of the kind for many years that I know of is one entry in some church-wardens' accounts of the time of Mary, belonging to the parish of Cheswardine, Salop.[1] It runs "for a forme to serve in procession tyme." This "forme," I have no doubt, was a thing for the priest and others to kneel at when singing the "procession" or litany.]

THE CARECLOTH. This was a sort of veil which was held over the heads of a newly-married couple when they received the blessing. There does not appear to have been any rule as to its material.[2]

THE PASTE. This was scarcely an ecclesiastical ornament. It was a sort of coronet worn by brides at weddings; and it appears that some parishes had them and let them out at a regular charge to those who wanted them. The parish of St. Margaret, Westminster, bought one in 1540 for £4 10s., as appears by the parish books.

[1] Quoted by the Rev. J. T. Fowler, in the *Church Times*, 7 Dec. 1883. Some may, perhaps, think it strange to find this note in the time of Queen Mary. But it should be remembered that, on the accession of Mary, the return was made not to the state of things before the beginning of the Reformation, but to that at the death of Henry VIII. when scarcely anything remained to be done in the way of real reform, except the translation of the services into English. There was a Roman party at Court, and to it we owe the persecution which has made the name of Mary unpopular; but such men as Gardiner and Tonstal had been leading reformers, and although the excesses of the puritan faction in Edward's time drove them now to accept the authority of the Bishop of Rome, there is no reason for believing that they had changed in a desire for reform. It is at least significant that, of all the shrines which had been taken down in Henry's time, the only one known to have been set up again in Mary's was at Westminster Abbey, a now royal foundation.

[2] The Guild of St. Mary at Boston in Lincolnshire, which concerned itself much with the services of the church, and owned all the ornaments necessary to furnish them, possessed in 1534 "a care cloth of silke dornex conteynynge in leynth iij yardes and a quarter and in brede one yarde." (Peacock's *Church Furniture*, p. 204.)

The price is considerable, and in 1562 the thing is described as "set with pearl and stone." About the same time mention is made of one at St. Lawrence's, Reading, and another at Steyning, in Sussex.[1]

OTHER WEDDING GEAR. Some churches possessed other things for use at weddings which scarcely need notice, as they were not properly church ornaments, and the possession of them depended chiefly upon the accident of their having been given to the churches. Some of them had reference to usages general at weddings, and would be found by the parties concerned where the churches lacked them. Of such was the silver cup given in 1534 "to be carried before all brydds that were wedded in St Laurence Church" at Reading.[2] The ceremonial drinking together in church at the end of the wedding service was a recognised custom, and the cup was formally blessed by the priest. The note in the Reading parish books shows us that the cup was carried into the church in the bride's procession, and her friends must have provided it if one had not been given for general use.

THE PYX. A PURSE TO PUT IT IN. THE BELL. THE LANTERN. These were used in taking the Sacrament to the sick. I believe that in poor parishes the priest took the pyx which ordinarily hung over the altar, but in most a special one was used. And it appears from an inventory of the goods of St. Mary's church, Sandwich, that sometimes a cup for the drink given after Communion was in some way fitted to it.[3] The pyx was often, though perhaps not always, carried in a little bag or purse.[4] The bell and lantern were carried by the clerk, or, it might be, by two clerks, before the priest who bore the Sacrament.[5] The chrismatory has already been men-

---

[1] See *Sussex Archaeological Collections*, 1856. viii. 137; also *Diary of Henry Machyn*, Camden Society, p. 240; and Kerry's *St. Lawrence's Church, Reading*, p. 49.

[2] Kerry, *op. cit.* pp. 119, 120.

[3] "A cowpe of sylver and gylt for the sacrament with a lytill cuppe ther yn ygylt, to geve the seke body drynke ther of, xxix oz." (Boys's *History of Sandwich*, p. 374.)

[4] "Payd for sylk for mekyng off on purse for to bere the sakarament in to seke forlke vij^d. payd Alson fendyk for makyng off the same purse viij^{d}" *Churchwardens' accounts for the parish of Leverton in Lincolnshire* for 1544. (Printed by Mr. Edward Peacock in *Archaeologia*, 1867. xli. 356.) The sum paid for making must have included some embroidery or other ornament.

[5] "A litill bell that ryngeth afore the sacrament." (St. Michael Cornhill. 1469. p. 40.) "Two Lanterns, to go with a Visitation, and one of them is in decay." (Long Melford 1529. p. 19.)

D

tioned. It contained the oil for the sick, with the other two oils, it being the custom to keep all together.

A CROSS FOR FUNERALS. It was required that a church should have a special cross to be carried before the corpse at a funeral.

THE HANDBELL. This was rung before the funeral procession on its way to the church. It was also used for " crying " of obits, that is, giving notice of them abroad in the parish, and asking for prayers for the soul of the deceased.

THE BIER OR HERSE. THE COMMON COFFIN. THE HERSE CLOTH. TORCHES. STANDING CANDLESTICKS WITH LIGHTS. Each parish was bound to have a bier, and the other things were often kept in the church, and payment was made for the use of them by such as could afford it. Burial in a coffin was the exception, but many churches had one with a hinged lid, which used to be lent to bring bodies to the grave in.[1]

OTHER FUNERAL GEAR. In descriptive accounts of important funerals two special lights are often mentioned as the *white branches.* They were carried in the procession and placed upon the coffin during the services. Machyn, the diarist, who seems to have had a trade interest in such things, often mentions white branches. At York they used to lay a small cross upon the body at a funeral; and in 1409 the want of such a cross was thought serious enough to be presented at a visitation.[2] It is then spoken of as a local custom, but it was used in other places. The *herse,* as a canopy of curtains with many lights about it, was rather an undertaker's affair than an ornament of the church. It had grown to be a very extravagant thing,[3] and it was sometimes set up for *months minds* and other commemorative services as well as at the time of burial. The banners and heralds' stuff

---

[1] This custom was long kept up, and even yet a common coffin may sometimes be found stowed away in an old church. I lately saw one of the 17th century at Howden, in Yorkshire, and I have heard of others.

[2] York, St. Michael-le-Belfrey: "Non habent parvas cruces ad iacendum super feretra mortuorum, prout moris est civitatis." (*York Fabric Rolls,* p. 247.)

[3] At the funeral of John Paston, at Bromholm, in 1466, the glass had to be taken out of two lights of the windows, to let the smoke out. (*Paston Letters,* Ed. J. Gairdner, 1874. ii. 268.) This was the funeral of a country gentleman only. A well known instance is furnished by the drawing of the funeral of Abbot Islip in Westminster abbey in 1532. (*Vetusta Monumenta,* iv. plate xviii.)

THE ORNAMENTS OF THE RUBRIC. 51

generally were only matters of worldly pomp, and therefore the puritans did not object to them, in the same way that they did to the ancient ornaments of the Church.[1]

It was the custom to lay a cloth or pall over a grave inside a church until the gravestone or tomb was made and often to place lights at the head and foot.[2] Sometimes there were endowments to keep up lights round tombs, but these had been confiscated by the Act 1st Edward VI. cap. 14.

THE CANOPY FOR PROCESSIONS. This was a canopy carried on four staves above the Sacrament in processions.[3] The procession on Corpus Christi day, with other usages belonging to particular seasons, was being put down in 1548. They were forbidden, but, so far as I can find, not in a way that can be said to have had the authority of Parliament; and it seems that this year the prohibition had not yet taken effect generally, except where the direct influence of the Court was strong. I therefore include the canopy and some other things similarly affected in the list of ornaments retained in the second year of King Edward. They appear to have been used in most churches in 1548, in many in 1549, but not generally after that.

TORCH STAVES AND TORCHES FOR PROCESSIONS. To carry before the Sacrament.[4]

CANDLE HOLDER. In the procession at Candlemas each person carried a candle in his or her hand, and some had sockets or holders wherein to place them. Now and then

---

[1] The funeral of Oliver Cromwell is a notable example of pompous extravagance.

[2] Amongst his "avaylis" or perquisites the clerk of St. Nicholas's church, Bristol, was "to have ye herse cloth when any such fall that is kept uppon the grave durynge the month w¹ ij lampis on at the fete and the tother at the hed of grave as the usage ys." Howe the Clerke and the Suffrigan, &c. quoted before (p. 86 s.)

[3] Wing Church, Buckinghamshire, had in 1547, "a clothe for the canopey off maytteyn, the coler of vyolett, wyth foore stavys unto the same." (*Archaeologia*, 1855. xxxvi. 222.) In 1486 at St. Margaret Pattens there were "iiij Stavys paynted ffor the Canapye w¹ corpus x'pi uppon theym And w⁴ iiij. angell₃ gilt to stand uppon theym." (*Archaeological Journal*, xlii. 322.) A later mention of the same canopy describes it as "servyng for Corpus x'pi day." (p. 329.) The canopy belonging to St. Christopher's le Stocks is described as "a cloth of gold, fyne bawdekyn, with a valance aboute of silke, called a Vertame, that serveth to bere over the sacrement, with iiij. staves and iiij. bellis longyng therto." (p. 115.)

[4] "There bith vi Judas Staves for torches peynted, havyng iche a castell gilded to set inne torchetts to bere with the Sacrement on Corpus Cristy daye and other tymes." (Inventory of St. Christopher's le Stocks, 1488. p. 119.)

we find in a list of church goods one of these provided for the use of the priest.[1]

THE LENTEN VEIL OR LENT CLOTH. A curtain generally of blue or white or of the two "paned" together, which was drawn across the chancel before the altar in Lent.[2]

OTHER CLOTHS FOR LENT. It was the custom to cover up the great rood and all pictures and images during Lent, and entries of sheets or cloths for the purpose are common in inventories. Sometimes these cloths were stained or embroidered with devices bearing reference to the subject they were intended to veil. The cross carried in processions was veiled like the rest, as appears by the York order that it should be *nudata* on Easter Even, already quoted, which implies that it had lately been otherwise. The two *lawns for the cross*[3] in the inventory of St. Saviour's Church, Southwark, in 1548, were I believe for this use.

THE EASTER SEPULCHRE. This, though only set up for a short time each year, was often an elaborate and costly structure, and, to judge from the many gifts for its adornment, it would seem that of all the ceremonies of Passiontide that of the Sepulchre most deeply affected the minds of the people. The name sepulchre is sometimes given to the altar or other place at which in modern Continental churches the Sacrament is specially reserved from the Mass of Maundy Thursday to that of Good Friday. But the old English Sepulchre was quite different and was used at a different time. With us the Sacrament remained suspended over the altar as usual until the Mass of the Pre-Sanctified on Good Friday, and then It was taken down and carried in the pyx solemnly to the Sepulchre, and there shut up together with the cross. So It remained until early on Easter morning

---

[1] "A thyng to ber' holy candle in on Candlemasse day for the priest." (St. Margaret Pattens, London, about 1500, p. 325.) "Item .j. candelabrum argenteum deauratum cum longo manubrio pro die purificationis beate Marie." (All Souls' College, Oxford, 1448. A.D. p. 122.)

[2] In 1552 the church of Boxford, Berkshire, had "a lent vayle before the highe awlter w⁴ paynes blewe and white." (Walter Money, *Parish Church Goods in Berkshire*, Parker, Oxford, 1879, p. 6.) Sometimes the hooks to which the wire or cord on which the veil ran may be found in the walls or pillars of a church, as at the cathedrals of Salisbury and Ripon. There is an example in a country parish church at Shillington, Bedfordshire.

[3] "ij lawnes for the crosse the one blewe the other white frenged both with golde." (Tyssen, *Surrey Inventories*, p. 82.)

when the Sepulchre was opened and the Sacrament carried in triumphant procession round the church and finally replaced over the altar. These ceremonies were intended to show forth the death, burial, and resurrection of our Lord. And it is evident that they did so very powerfully. The Sepulchre was hung about with curtains and decked with other ornaments, as to which custom varied greatly in different churches. So long as it was in use, the Sepulchre was surrounded by many lights, and was continually watched. The passage quoted in a note below[1] tells of a custom to leave the Sepulchre standing till the Thursday in Easter week. When empty it became a fitting trophy of the Resurrection. In a note to the paragraph on the pyx I have expressed a doubt whether the structures at Heckington and Hawton and simpler ones of the like sort such as that at Navenby, which are generally called Easter sepulchres, are not rather "Sacrament houses." And I believe that the sepulchre proper, that is, the casket, or whatever it may have been, in which the Sacrament was deposited, was something which could be taken away when the season for its use was over. But there often was a permanent structure in or on which this sepulchre was placed. Sometimes we know it was a tomb with a flat top, and sometimes it was an architectural composition of some size and importance. There is a very fine one in the church of St. Mary le Crypt, Gloucester, on the north side of the high altar; and opposite to it is a curious squint by which it could be watched from the south chapel.

THE TRIANGULAR CANDLESTICK. Called also the *Herse* the *Harrow* and the *Judas*.[2] It was used to put the

---

[1] In 1509 Alice Bray left to the church of Chelsfield "a taper iij li. wax to bren before the sepulture of ouer lorde w' in the said church at the tyme of Easter that is to saye from goode fridaye to thursdaye in the Ester weke to be brennyng at times conuenyant according as other ligthes be wonte and used to be kept there about the sepulture." (Cited by Mr. Leland L. Duncan in the *Transactions of the St. Paul's Ecclesiological Society*, 1895. iii. 260.)

[2] "In uno Judas de novo facto pro candel tenebrarum." (Church Accounts for 1427-8 in Dymond's *History of St. Petrock's, Exeter*, p. 410.) The word *Judas* has been laid hold of by some people and appropriated to mean a sham candle, and in an odd way the existence of the word has been made an excuse for the sham. It may be true that *Judas* in old writings does sometimes mean a sham candle, but not often; and I do not believe that an instance can be found in which it is used, as it generally is now, for a wooden candle to be put on an altar. It is used for the herse light as above, for a staff with a "castle" on the top

candles on during the office of *Tenebræ* on the three last days of Holy Week.

THE PASCHAL CANDLESTICK. Every parish church seems to have had this in the form either of a large standing candlestick of wood or metal or of a bason hanging from the roof,[1] or, I believe, sometimes not hanging. Its place was on the north side of the presbytery.[2]

BANNERS. Banners, standards, and streamers in various forms were used to deck the churches and carried in processions. Banners seem at first to have specially belonged to the Rogation processions, but were afterwards used in those of Corpus Christi and others. Two of the Rogation-tide banners are ordered by the rubrics in the processionals to bear respectively a lion and a dragon, and the dragon was often, and perhaps generally, not painted on a cloth but represented by a figure carried on a staff. Other banners bore various devices; figures of saints, coats of arms, badges, and sometimes texts. I have mentioned the custom of hanging one to the cross. Sometimes they used to fly a flag from the steeple on feasts.[3]

---

to carry a torch in procession, and for a wooden core or stiffener round which the paschal candle was cast. The word is curious, and needs explanation. It seems to have been used indifferently for any moveable wooden thing made to set a candle or candles upon.

[1] The hanging bason was a London fashion; but we sometimes meet it elsewhere. "A bason of peauter w^t iiij small square bollys for the Pascall" (St. Margaret Pattens, 1470. p. 315.) "Payed for the Pascall bason and the hangyng of the same xviij^s. Item payed for vij pendaunts for the same bason and the caryage from London iij^s." (St. Lawrence's, Reading, 1498. p. 51.) In Mr. Peacock's Lincolnshire inventories the paschal *post* is often mentioned. I take it to have been a wooden candlestick standing on the ground, or perhaps fixed in it.

[2] According to the direction in the Sarum Processional the first to be lighted from the new fire on Easter Even was "*cereum . . . de tribus candelis tortis in unum in ima parte conjunctis et insuper ab invicem divisis super quandam hastam.* (*Processionale ad usum insignis ac praeclarae Ecclesiae Sarum*, ed. Henderson, Leeds, 1882. p. 74.) This was carried to the quire for the lighting of the Paschal candle. Such a triple candle would be troublesome to make and therefore costly and there is some evidence that when the ceremony of the new fire was done in a parish church they were content to use three small candles fixed separately on to anything which they might have convenient for carrying them. Thus at St. Stephen's Walbrook about 1480 we find a payment of twelve pence for "Judas candyll and crosse candill." (p. 348.) Here "Judas candyll" means the small tapers for the triangular candlestick and "crosse candill," I believe, three like tapers for the new fire fixed upon the top of a cross, which may have been the lenten processional cross then just about to be put away for the year. At Stratton in Cornwall in 1558 a penny was paid "for candyles to put uppon the banner staffe," (*Archaeologia*, 1881. xlvi. 225.) which seems to be another makeshift of the same kind.

[3] "For a baner for the stepill agenst our dedycacion day xiijd. ob." (Boys's *Sandwich*, p. 364.)

VERGES. In collegiate and, so long as they remained, in monastic churches, it was usual for servants bearing tipped staves or verges to go before processions and the clergy as they approached the altars.[1] And although no positive proof of it appears, it is most likely that the same was done in the more important parish churches, and that the use of the verge, which exists in some of them at the present time, is an ancient tradition.

WANDS. The wand is a very ancient badge of office. In the middle ages it was carried by officers of the crown, sheriffs, mayors of towns, and others; and when we find it still used by churchwardens as chief officers of the parish, it is safe to infer that they have it from their predecessors of the remote past; although the small value of the wand itself, and the accident that it was not connected with any usage which was matter of debate in the sixteenth century, have kept the mention of it out of inventories and other documents. The wands in traditional use till lately were of wood, either quite plain and unpainted, which is probably the most ancient form, or painted white, with a few inches at the top blue or gilt. Coloured and varnished wands with fantastical devices in brass or white metal on the tops have not been in use more than forty years.

THE DEDICATION CROSSES. The oldest English pontifical, that of Egbert, Archbishop of York, does not directly mention the dedication crosses, but it does mention the candles which we find associated with them in later times, though only those on the outside of the church, and also it directs the bishop to make crosses with the chrism on the walls round-about the church inside.[2] It is therefore probable that the custom of that early time did not vary greatly from what we

[1] "*Deinde eat processio hoc ordine. In primis procedant ministri virgam manu gestantes locum facientes processioni*, &c." (Rubric in Sarum *Processional*, p. 5.) "When the office of the masse began to be sung the Epistoler came out of the revestrie and the other two monkes following him, all three arow, at the south Quire dore, and there did stand untill the *Gloria Patri* of the office of the masse began to bee sunge, and then, with great reverence and devotion, they went all upp to the High Altar (and on of the vergers that kept the vestrie did goe before them, with a tipt staffe in his hand, as it was his office so to doe)" (*Rites of Durham*, Surtees Society, 1842. p. 7.)

[2] "*Illuminentur duodecim candelae, et ponantur de foris per circuitum aecclesiae*" (*Pontifical of Egbert, Archbishop of York*, Surtees Society, 1853. p. 27.) and later: "*In circuitu aecclesiae per parietes de dextra in dextro faciens crucem cum pollice de ipso chrismate*" (p. 40.)

know it to have been for many years before the date of our enquiry, when twelve crosses were placed outside and as many inside, to mark the places anointed by the bishop at the consecration.¹ Many of these crosses still remain in our old churches, although the "restorers" in their excoriating zeal have destroyed many more. The painted are the most common, but carved examples are found. Those at Salisbury Cathedral Church are well known; as are those at Ottery St. Mary, which are held by figures of angels. Sometimes the crosses have been inlaid with metal, as some at Salisbury. Occasionally the cross under the east window was developed into a panel with a group of the crucifixion as at Coggeshall in Essex, and Chiseldon in Wilts. I think the prescribed number of crosses was not always exactly kept to.² There are remains of the iron brackets which held the candles below each of the crosses at Ottery St. Mary, outside as well as inside; and traces of them may be seen in the Chapel of Henry VII. and other places.

BELLS IN THE STEEPLE. THE CLOCK AND CHIMES. A parish church was to be provided, not with a bell, but with bells, and even the smallest had two. Chapels sometimes had one bell only. Rich churches had "tuneable" sets of bells, though they were not rung *up* as was done fifty years later. Clocks and chimes playing on the bells were not very uncommon.³

CLAPPERS. The returns of church goods in Lincolnshire in Elizabeth's time, printed by Mr. Peacock in his *Church Furniture*, often include clappers or claps.⁴ They

---

¹ The rubric at the beginning of the office for the consecration of a church in the pontifical of Archbishop Christopher Bainbridge of York orders that there be got ready beforehand: *Duodecim cruces pictae foris et duodecim intus; viginti quatuor cereoli et totidem clavi quibus cereoli infigantur, duodecim foris et duodecim intus super singulas cruces.* (*Liber Pontificalis Chr. Bainbridge Archiepiscopi Eboracensis*, Surtees Society, 1875. p. 53.)

² Often a small cross may be found cut on one of the jambs of a doorway, generally but not always the east jamb of a south doorway. I believe that this is an addition to the ordinary dedication crosses, just as the cross sometimes found in the middle of the front edge of an altar slab is an addition to the usual five on the top. We know that the extra cross on the altar slab marks a place that was anointed by itself, and I suspect that the cross on the door jamb does so also, though the rubrics do not mention it.

³ John Baret, whose will has already been quoted with respect to chimes inside the church, also left money for the repair of those in the steeple of his parish church, and desired that they should play *Requiem Eternam* at certain times in memory of him. (*Bury Wills*, p. 29.)

⁴ Pages 43, 118, 126, 188, &c.

were things to make a noise with on the three last days of Holy Week, when by custom the church bells were not used. Their use is very ancient, and it is found also in the Eastern Church. But there is not evidence to prove that it was general in English parish churches in the sixteenth century. I am not sure what a clapper was like here,[1] but I think it was a board hung up by a loop and struck with a mallet. A like machine was used in monastic cloisters. At Rouen they used a horn instead of bells in Holy Week,[2] and so many customs were common to England and Normandy that I should not be surprised to learn that the same was sometimes done here. But I have not found proof of it yet.

FIRE PANS. THE CHAFING BALL. Fire pans were kept in vestries chiefly to supply embers for the censers,[3] but sometimes they were put in the church in cold weather. The idea of warming a whole church is a very modern one.[4] Of old, men used to protect themselves from cold by putting on extra clothing. But for the celebrating priest, lest his hands should become numbed with cold, so that he could not properly use them, there was sometimes provided a thing like the muff-warmer which ladies use now.[5] It was warmed with water or with a heated ball.

CRESSETS. CANDLES FOR LIGHT. Except at the service at midnight or very early in the morning on Christmas Day, for which we find candles regularly provided,[6] a

---

[1] They were of wood, as some are recorded to have been burned.

[2] De Vert, *Explication . . . des Cérémonies de l'Église*, 2nd edition, 1709, i. 51.

[3] "*Solutum Willielmo Hunte pro factura de le fyrpanne*" is an item in the churchwarden's accounts of Bishops Stortford for a period of nine years ending in 1540. (Glasscock, p. 10.)

[4] There is a letter in the *Gentleman's Magazine* for 1755 (p. 68) in which stoves in churches are mentioned as a novelty much to be commended. The earliest example I have found of any provision for warming having been made at the building of a church is at St. John's, Wakefield, which was built about 1795. In making some alterations there a few years ago, I found that there had been two open fireplaces in the outer corners of the aisles at the west end. They were far under the gallery, and can have done very little towards warming people in pews, the tops of which were above the tops of the fireplaces. They had long ago been superseded, and were plastered over and forgotten.

[5] "j chawfyng ball de auricalco." (Finchale in 1481. p. 137.) "A Rounde balle of laton and gilte, and a litle balle therin of Irne, In Colde wedyr to make yt brennyng hote, and then put hit Inne the balle for a preat to have hit in his hande In wyntir." (St. Stephen's Walbrook c. 1480. p. 340.)

[6] I give, from amongst many examples, two chosen for their late date from the accounts of the Church of St. Helen, Abingdon, printed in Nichols's *Illustrations* (p. 142.) 1561. 4th Eliz.: "Payde for four pounds of candilles upon Christmas in the morning for the masse." 1574. 16th Eliz. "Payde for candilles for the church at Christmas."

parish church seems never to have been lighted up. The ordinary services were said by daylight, except the earliest Masses in winter, and at them the worshippers did not need to read, so that a light or two to guide them on entering the church would serve. In quires where the night office was kept we know that they used to put cressets or mortars[1] at doors and corners where people had to pass, and there is proof that the like was sometimes done in parish churches in a stone with seven cressets, which does, or did very lately, stand on a base inside the north door of that at Lewanick, in Cornwall. I have seen such stones in other parish churches, but not one which, like this, appeared to be in its original position. It is not uncommon to find a lantern hanging in the body of the church mentioned in inventories, and this may have been to give light.[2] In the north wall of the west tower of Blakeney Church, Norfolk, is a recess with six holes in two rows, evidently intended to hold candles to light people coming in at the door near by; and it was very likely usual to put a light in such a place. But if there had been any general lighting up, the churchwardens' accounts would contain some record of it, which, with the exception just mentioned, they do not. When it was dark in the church it was dark out of doors, and folk who wanted light would bring their lanterns.[3]

Now as to the ornaments of the ministers. By "ministers" here are meant all who minister about the service, from the Archbishop to the humblest clerk. But as before, I shall keep chiefly to the things which would be used in a parish church.

THE CASSOCK. THE PRIEST'S CAP. THE AMYS. THE TIPPET. THE BLACK COPE. These things were not kept by the churches, as they were part of the ordinary clerical dress of the time, and the surplice might almost have been included with them, as most clerks wore their

---

[1] They were cups of stone, metal, or earthenware, which were filled with grease, and a wick set to burn in each. For examples see two papers in the *Archæological Journal*, 1882. xxxix. one (p. 890) by the Rev. T. Lees, the other (p. 896) by Sir Henry Dryden.

[2] "ij lanternes one of glasse in the body of the churche and other of horne for palme sondaye" (St. Peter's Cornhill, 1546. p. 281.)

[3] I was told lately at Sidbury, in Devonshire, that a few years ago only the pulpit and reading desk were lighted up in the church there, and on dark afternoons in winter people used to bring their own lights.

own and came to church in them, as they still do at the Universities. The priest's cap has its modern representative in the square college cap, which is directly derived from it by a gradual process of stiffening. The *biretta* is a foreign degradation of the same sort, and I can not understand why, when we have our own tradition, we should go out of our way to adopt a foreign one. If the modern English form is thought not to be suitable for use in church, the change should be to that in use at the date to which the rubric refers us. The cap was used in processions and in quire,[1] but not at the altar.

The amys was a fur hood with a cape, orginally intended to keep the wearer warm. Later it became a badge of dignity, and distinctions were made in its material and form.

The tippet, which has been thought by some to be only a variety of the amys, was a scarf generally of black silk, sometimes lined with fur. It has a curious later history. It was retained by dignitaries, who wore it, as they still do, in quire. Bishop Blomfield, of London, for some reason wished all his clergy to use it, and from them it spread to other dioceses. Then it came to be called a stole, and that soon led to its being made like one. Thus it comes that the stole is now generally used, though sixty years ago it was as obsolete as the chasuble was.

The black cope was a gown without sleeves, partly open in front, but otherwise quite close. It was generally of black stuff, and was worn over the surplice in quires at certain times. I do not know of any direct evidence of its use in parish churches, but it probably was used there sometimes.

TUCKING GIRDLES. Sometimes a priest found it convenient to gird up his cassock or other habit before assuming the vestments, and girdles were kept in vestries for this use. They were used by seculars as well as regulars.[2]

---

[1] The custom of covering the head in church was much commoner in the middle ages than it is now. The change was one of many which resulted from the struggle between the Church and the Puritans in the seventeenth century. The Puritans abused the liberty, so Churchmen set themselves against it, and in the end succeeded in stopping it.

[2] At Leverton in 1521 " *pro zonis ad cingendos presbyteros ad missam et pro latoppe iijd. ob.*" (p. 347.) And again in 1528 " for tuckyng gurdylles to wer at messe ijd." (p. 351.) In the direc-

THE AMICE. THE ALB.[1] THE GIRDLE. THE STOLE. THE FANON OR MANIPLE. THE CHASUBLE. These made up what was called a single vestment. Every parish church was bound to possess one, and I think they generally did possess at least three, which were assigned according to their quality, and often with little regard to their colour, to festal, ferial and penitential times respectively. A full vestment included also

THE DALMATIC AND THE TUNICLE with amices, albs, girdles and fanons for the gospeller and epistoler, and a stole for the gospeller. Churches which could afford them were bound to have these also, and rich churches had many. A suit or vestment often included other things besides these, as a cope or several copes, vestments and curtains for the altar, vestments for servers, and a cloth for the lectern.

COPES. Silk copes were worn by the clergy in processions and for the censing of the altars at mattins and evensong on feasts. They did not wear them all through the office; but the custom seems to have been to lay the cope upon the altar before the service and take it thence before the censing. Churches in which the ceremonial ruling of the choir was used had also copes for the two or sometimes four " standers," who wore them at Mass, as well as at mattins and evensong.

By way of distinction from the black cope, (*capa nigra*,) the ceremonial cope is called in the rubrics *capa serica*, but it was often made of material other than silk, especially in poor churches.

The Morse was an appendage to the cope, which was, I think, not often found in parish churches. It had originally been a real clasp by which the cope was closed in the front, but by the sixteenth century it had become a merely ornamental brooch of goldsmith's work, which was fastened to the front band.

It may be well here to mention the *Rationale*, which is

tions for laying things out ready for the Abbot of Westminster to vest there was provided "a vestry girdle to tukk up bys coll [cowl]." (*Archaeologia*, 1890. lii. 214.)

[1] The alb was properly of linen, but the inventories of great churches often include silk albs, and the way they are sometimes classed and described (as in the Westminster Abbey inventory taken in 1388 and printed by Dr. Wickham Legg in *Archaeologia*, 1890. lii. 241) shows that they were really silk vestments, and not linen ones with ornaments of silk.

included in some lists professing to be of the Edwardian ornaments. I do not know an English name for it, nor any evidence of its ever having been used in an English parish church. It was one of several ornaments affected by prelates in the twelfth century in imitation of the Aaronic high priests. But the fashion does not seem to have generally lasted long.

SURPLICES. ROCHETS. Three surplices[1] and a rochet are included in the list of things to be provided by the parishioners, set forth by Archbishop Robert Winchelsea of Canterbury in 1305. And Lyndewode's note on the rochet is "*Rochetum . . . differt a superpelliceo. quia superpelliceum habet manicas pendulas. sed rochetum est sine manicis et ordinatur pro clerico ministraturo sacerdoti vel forsan ad opus ipsius sacerdotis in baptizando pueros ne per manicas ipsius brachia impediantur.*"[2] In quires, or at least in those of old foundation, clerks ministering at the altar used albs, but in parish churches the rochet was generally used. It was sleeved sometimes, but its sleeves were close and not hanging like those of a surplice. In great quires servers used to be vested in tunicles, and sometimes in copes.[3] But I do not think these were worn by them in parish churches. Such vestments described as "for children" are not uncommon in parish inventories. Sometimes it is said that they are for St. Nicholas's bishop, and probably they all were so. That sport was very popular in the middle of the sixteenth century, and ornaments of considerable value were given for it.[4]

[1] It appears from the following passage from a tract printed in London in 1534, that silk surplices were a vanity occasionally indulged in by secular canons. "Afterwardes do come in our masters and lordes of the close couered with gray amyces, and hauynge on a very white surples, but not suche one as the forsayde chaplaynes do weare, but of moste fyne raynes or sylke." (*A worke entytled of ye olde god and the newe*, Imprynted at London in Fletestrete by me Iohan Byddell, 1534. There is no pagination; but the passage may be found in sheet L, on its last page. The tract is a translation from the German.) When surplices are mentioned in inventories, which is not very often, special ones of better make are sometimes named for the parson of the parish; for example at St. Peter's Cornhill in 1546 "to viij^t prests clerk and Sexton viij^t surplisses. Item ij gathered surplesses for the parishe prest. Item vij surplesses for children for the quier." (p. 281.)

[2] Gloss of Lyndewode upon the word *rochetum* in *Ut parochiani* (*Provinciale*, lib. iii. *de ecclesiis edificandis*, cap. ii. fo. clxxxii.b.)

[3] For example of both at York Minster see *Fabric Rolls*, pp. 228, 233, and 234. They had sets of four tunicles *pro thuribulariis et choristis* in each of the four colours white, red, blue, and green.

[4] Another custom, which, though it was more directly connected with the

These then are the ornaments in use in the Church of England by authority of Parliament in the Second Year of King Edward the Sixth. There are some amongst them which are in abeyance, because the usages with which they were connected are not provided for in our present formularies. Of these it may be said that the "time of ministration" for which they were appointed does not occur now. But the most in number, the most ancient, and the most important can be used as well with our present services as they could with those of 1548 or 1549. And so let us use them, and not any novelties, English or foreign, instead of them. The substitution of foreign ornaments is mischievous from the countenance which it gives to those who profess to see in the present revival within the Church of England only an imitation of the Church of Rome. And we do not want the things, our own are better.

church service than that of the child bishop, scarcely deserves more notice, was that of dressing up a man or a boy in a fancy costume to represent a prophet and to meet the procession on Palm Sunday when a part to be sung was assigned to him. He was taken quite seriously and well-to-do churches kept things for his use, the most essential of which seem to have been a bat and a beard.

APPENDIX BY THE COMMITTEE.

In the opinion of the undersigned members of the Committee, all who were present at the discussion of this part of the paper, the paragraphs on THE TABLE OR REREDOS, on THE ALTAR SHELF, and on THE UPPER FRONTAL OR DORSAL, (p. 23.) should be read together, as follows:

THE UPPER FRONTAL, THE TABLE, HALPAS, OR REREDOS. Most frequently the reredos retained its earliest form of a curtain. It was then commonly called the upper frontal, and was a cloth of more or less richness hung against the wall above the altar, and of much the same size as the front of the altar itself. But often the upper frontal gave place to a reredos, of similar dimensions, made of wood or stone, and covered with imagery and painting. It was then commonly called the table. Less frequently the top of this table was used as a shelf, upon which to set the jewels, *i.e.* reliquaries and images. And when used in this way we find the reredos mentioned by different and various names. An inventory of goods of the Church of St. Christopher le Stock, in 1488, (p. 114.) has a *forme uppon the high altar undre the juellis*, and Holinshed, describing Henry VIII.'s Chapel on the Field of the Cloth of Gold, mentions the thing as an *halpas*[1], which means a high step, and again as a *deske*. Sometimes it would appear to have been a kind of cupboard, similar to some reredoses still to be seen in Germany. An inventory of goods belonging to the Church of St. Stephen, Coleman Street, mentions *iiij. coffins to ly on the auters*, which may have been in the form of reredoses.[2] Sometimes the front of the halpas was covered by the upper frontal. For example, an inventory of goods belonging to the Church

---

[1] In the accounts of St. Lawrence, Reading, of 1518, it is mentioned as *the Halpas wt the xij Appostels*. (C. Kerry, *History of the Municipal Church of St. Lawrence, Reading*, Reading, 1883, p. 27.)

[2] See, *e.g.* a reredos now set in front of another, and used as a shelf, at Xanten; and another reredos similar to it, but remaining in its original position beneath a triptych at Calcar. Both of these are "*coffins*," or cupboards, having doors at the ends; but in every other respect they resemble the usual reredos.

of St. Mary at Hill, in 1485, records *a frontell for the schelffe standyng on the altar.* The destruction of ancient altars has been so general that the survival of moveable ornaments, like the halpas, is hardly to be expected; but there are pictures in contemporary MSS.[1] answering to the descriptions of them in the inventories, and from these pictures it may be seen that the halpas is only to be distinguished from the usual reredoses by the images, or reliquaries, which are shown standing upon it, and that the two altar lights were not set upon it, but are invariably shown standing upon the altar itself, without intervention of any kind of shelf.

Notwithstanding the opinion often expressed that one of the secular courts has forbidden the setting of the candlesticks directly on the table of the altar, it seems hard to find any real ground for the statement. Sir Walter Phillimore writes to one of us: "No Court has decided that it is illegal to put candlesticks directly on the *mensa.*"

J. WICKHAM LEGG,
   Chairman.
W. J. BIRKBECK.
H. B. BRIGGS.
J. N. COMPER.
LELAND L. DUNCAN.

W. H. ST. JOHN HOPE.
W. H. H. JERVOIS.
T. A. LACEY.
G. H. PALMER.
ATHELSTAN RILEY.

---

[1] See, *e.g.* British Museum, Sloane MS. 2468, fol. 115, in which three images appear above an upper frontal which covers the halpas, and two candles stand upon the altar in front of it. See also Tib. A. vij. fol. 68, showing the typical long English altar. In this miniature the reredos takes the form of a low shelf, upon which stand six images. The middle is cut out to allow the cross to stand upon the altar itself. Behind the cross and six attendant images is an upper frontal, and close above them is a canopy corresponding to the shelf, or base, upon which the images stand, so that the appearance of the whole is that of the usual reredos. For other examples, viz. a halpas with reliquaries, and a halpas with an image standing upon it, see Paul Lacroix, *Vie Militaire et Religieuse au Moyen Age,* deuxième édition, Paris, 1873, p. 261, Fig. 200, and p. 425, Fig. 297.

INDEX.

Abingdon, 57*n*.
Alban's, St. Abbey, 28*n*.
Albe, 60.
  silk, 60*n*, 39*n*.
All Souls', Oxford,
  candlestick, 52*n*.
  corporas case, 34*n*.
Alms dishes, 39, 32*n*.
Altar, 22, 23.
  four in 1567, 28*n*.
  minor, 22.
  of stone, post reformation, 22*n*, 25*n*.
  of wood, 22*n*, 35*n*.
Altar bread box, 34.
  candlesticks, 31, 33.
  cards, 33.
  cover, 28.
  cross, 30.
  linen, 30.
Altar lights, modern extravagant multiplication, 43*n*.
  around, not on altar, 32.
  rail, 39, 23*n*.
  shelf, 23, 23*n*, 24*n*.
  appendix by committee on, 63.
  table, 23.
Amice, 60.
Amys, 59.
Apostles, images of, 32*n*, 63*n*.
Artificial flowers, 33*n*.
Ashes on Ash Wednesday, 18.
Authorities, list of, 9.

Banner, 54.
  for Easter, 37.
  for rogations, 54, 21*n*.
  Heralds' banners, 60.
  staff, 54.
Baptistery, foreign to England, 46.
Baret, John, 36, 56*n*.
Barnes, 37*n*.
Basons, 39, 32*n*, 46*n*.
Beam light, 43*n*.
Beard for prophet, 62*n*.
Becon, Thomas, *Displaying of the Popish Mass*, 21*n*.
Bells, 56.
  carried before sacrament, 49.
  certain use of, forbidden, 20.
  funeral, 50.
  sackering, 36.
  to be found by parish, 21*n*.

Beverley, stone altar at, 22*n*.
  copes, 44*n*.
Beylham, John, 43*n*.
Bible, 20, 45.
Bier, 50.
  to be found by parish, 21*n*.
Birchall, Rev. O. 25*n*.
Biretta, 59.
Bishops Stortford.
  fire pan, 57*n*.
  shriving house, 47*n*.
  trendyll, 35*n*.
Blakeney, 58.
Books, 32, 45, 45*n*.
  cushion for mass book, 32.
  desk, 45, 32.
  to be found by parish, 21*n*.
Bosham, 34*n*.
Boston, William, 23*n*.
Boston (town).
  care cloth, 48*n*.
  register, 36*n*.
  shriving cloth, 47*n*.
  skins for altar, 27*n*.
  sudary, 35*n*.
Bousfield, Rev. E. H., 36*n*.
Boxford, 52*n*.
Boy bishop, 61.
Bramble, Colonel, 37*n*.
Brand's *Popular Antiquities*, 21*n*.
Bray, Alice, 53*n*.
Bristol, 36*n*, 40*n*, 51*n*.
Bromholm, 50*n*.
Bromley, 39*n*.
Bruges, Sir W. 32*n*.
Burford, 46*n*.
Bury, 36*n*.
Buscot, 30*n*.
Byschop, John, 30*n*.

Calcar, 63*n*.
Cambridge, Great St. Mary.
  chrismatory cloth, 35*n*.
  churching veil, shriving stool, 47*n*.
  sun for sacrament, 37*n*.
Candle,
  at baptism, 46.
  about altar, not on, 32.
  at least one for mass, 31*n*.
  extravagant use of, 32*n*, 50*n*.
  to be of wax, 31*n*.
Candlebeam, 43*n*.

E

Candleholder, 51.
  at Candlemas, 52n.
Candlesticks,
  altar, 31.
  for processions, 51, 36.
  funeral, 50.
  'Judas,' 53n.
  paschal, 54, 44.
  standing, 33, 31n.
  triangular, 53.
Canons, secular, 61n.
Canopy,
  for processions, 51.
  for pyx, 28, 28n, 25n.
  for weddings, 48.
  over altar, 25.
Canterbury, supposed baptistery at, 46.
  St. Dunstan's, churching veil, 47n.
Cap, priest's, 58.
Cards, altar, 33.
Care cloth, 48.
Carpet, 27.
  silk, of 1603, 26n.
Cassock, 58.
Castle, to carry torch, 53n, 51n.
Castor, 30n.
Censer, 35.
  to be found by parish, 21n.
Chaddesden, 40.
Chafing ball, 57.
Chalice, 33.
  making of, 41n.
  to be found by parish, 21n.
Chalice veil, silk, modern, 35.
Chanters' copes, 44.
  staves, 43.
  stools, 43.
Chantries, 19, 20n.
Charterhouse, 41.
Chasuble, 60.
  to be found by parish, 21n.
Chelsfield, 53n.
Chime cases, 36n.
Chimes, 36, 56.
Chiseldon, 56.
Choirs, see Quires.
Chrismatory, 46, 35, 49.
Christ Church, Hampstead, 28n.
Christmas, tree, 44n.
  extra candles at, 57n.
Christopher le Stocks, St.
  basons, 40.
  candlesticks, 31n.
  canopy and torches, 51n.
  cross, 31n.
  form for high altar, 24.
  lectern, 43n.
  library, 45n.
  sudary, 35n.
  superaltars, 35n.
Chrysom cloth, 47.
Churching cloth, 47.
Cistercians, 41.

Clappers, 56.
Clock in steeple, 56.
Closets, a shut up pew, 45.
Clun, 25, 28.
Cod, see cushion.
Coffer } for the Sacrament, 29.
Coffyn }
Coffin, common, 50.
Coffin on altar, 24, 29, 63.
Coggeshall, 56.
Cold Overton, 24.
Collecting dishes, 39n.
Collegiate churches, see Quires.
Colwyn, John, 30n.
Commandments, ten, tables of, 45.
Communion, Our Lady's, and Apostles, 23n.
Communion tables, 23.
Confessional, 47.
Cooke, Rev. William, 28n.
Cope, black, 58, 60.
  rich or silk, 60, 21, 44, 61.
Cope, choir, to be found by parish, 21n.
Cornhill, St. Peter's,
  wooden altar, 22n.
Corporas, 33, 34n.
Corporas case, 33, 34n, 28n.
Corpus Christi,
  canopy for, 51.
  garlands, on feast of, 33n.
  monstrance on, 37.
  pyx for, 29.
"Correctness," 13.
Costers, 27.
Credence, 40.
Cressets, 57.
Crewets, 34, 40, 41n.
Crich, 40.
Cromwell, Oliver, 51n.
Cross banner, 37.
  candle, 53.
  cloth, 37n.
  locker, 37.
Crosses, dedication, 55.
Cross for Lent, 37.
  foot, 30.
  on altar, 30.
  rood, 42.
  staff, 30.
  to be found by parish, 21n.
  to lay on corpse, 50n.
Cross, processional, 36, 30, 37.
  for funerals, 50.
  to be found by parish, 21n, 30.
Crucifix, 30, 22n, 42.
Cup at weddings, 49.
Curtains for altars, 27, 60.
  elevation, 26.
  shriving pew, 47.
Cushion, 32.
  as gradine, 24n.

Dalmatic, 60.

INDEX. 67

Dalmatic, to be found by parish, 21n.
Dedham, 43n.
Derby, All Saints', stone altar at, 22n.
  super altar, 36n.
Desk on altar, 32, 24.
  for books, 45.
  for Gospel, 40.
  for quire, 43.
Dignissimum eucharistiae, 28n.
Dishes, 32, 35, 39.
Doncaster, Deanery of, 38.
Dorsal, 25.
Dragon, rogation procession, 54.
Duncan, Mr. Leland L. notes from wills, 8, 31n, 39n, 53n.
Durham,
  monstrance, 38n.
  vergers, 55n.

Eagle desk, 40.
Eastern church, clappers, 57.
Easter Sepulchre, 52, 29n.
  monstrance for, 37n.
Edward VI, second year of, 16, 15, 20, 42, 62.
  reign, full of change, 17.
Egbert of York, 55n.
Elevation curtain, 26.
England, Church of, 15, 62.
Erasmus, Paraphrase of, 20, 45.
Ewer, 35, 46.
Ewer, bason, and napkin for baptisms, 46.
Ewerby, 29n.
Exeter, St. Kerrian, 30n.

Fanon, 60.
Faversham, pyx canopy, 28p.
'Feigned miracles,' 21.
Fertur, 38n.
Finchale,
  chafing ball, 57n.
  crewets, 34n.
Fire pan, 57.
Flag, 54.
Floor drain, 41n.
Flower pots, 33.
  vases not used, 33.
Flowers, not used to deck altars, 33n.
  artificial, 53n.
Font, 45, 35.
  cloth, 45.
  covers, 45.
  locker, 46n.
  to be found by parish, 21n.
Forel, 33, 34n.
Forme on altar, 24.
Fowler, Rev. J. T. 29n, 48n.
"Frame" for the Sacrament, 29.
Frontal, upper, 25, 62.
  for altar shelf, 24.
  nether, 26.
  to be found by the parish, 21n.
Frontlet, 26, 30.

Galleries, 42.
Gardiner, 48n.
Garlands of flowers, 33.
Girdle, 60.
  tucking, 59.
Gloucester altar rails, 23n.
Gloucester, 41n.
Goodewyn, Joan, 39n.
Googe, Barnaby, *Popish Kingdom*, 21n.
Goosey Church, 25.
Gospel book, 32.
Gradine, 23, 23n, 24n.
  appendix by committee on, 63.
Grantham, 24.
Gray's Inn, 35n.
Grene, Thomas, 30n.
Guilds, confiscation of property, 19.
Guisnes, 32n.

Haconby, 23n.
Hair, 25.
Halpas on altar, 24.
Hand bell, 36, 49, 50.
  to be found by parish, 21n.
Harrow, 53.
Hat for prophet, 62n.
Henry VII.'s chapel, 23n, 24, 25, 56.
Henry VIII.'s chapel at Guisnes, 24, 32n, 63.
Hereford, 45n.
Herse, 50, 53.
Herse light, 51.
Herto, Agas, 46n.
Hessett, Suffolk, 28n.
Hingeston-Randolph, 30n, 34n.
Holland, reservation in, 23n.
Holly bush, 41n.
Holme, William, 46n.
Holy bread, 38.
  candle, 38n, 52n.
  loaf, 38n.
  stock, 47.
  vat, 38.
  water sprinkle, 38.
Hoo, 47n.
Hope, Mr. W. H. St. John, extracts from inventories, 8, 27n.
Horns for bells in holy week, 57.
Houseling cloth, 38.
Howden, 50.
Hungate, St. John's church, 22n.

Images, 21, 23, 33n.
  apostles, 32n.
  superstitious, to be taken away, 19.
  to be found by parishioners, 21n.
Incense ship, 35.
Injunctions, 19, 20.
Inscriptions, 33, 45.
Inventories, list of, 9.
Irons in shriving house, 47.
Islip Roll, 25, 50.

Jack towel, 35.
Jewels, 24, 32n, 36, 38n.
Joye, Alice, 47n.
Judas, 53, 54n.
Judas candle, 53n.
Judas staves, 51n.

Kingston-upon-Thames, three communion tables, 23n.
King's Lynn, St. Margaret, 40.

Lady Chapels, 43.
Lamps, 29.
Lampstead, 30.
Lantern, 49, 58.
  to be found by parish, 21n.
Lavatory, 40.
Lawns for the cross, 52.
Lectern, cloth, 43, 60.
  great, 43.
Lecterns,
  for altar, 32.
  gospel, 49.
  music, 20.
  organ, 43n.
  quire, 43.
Legg, Dr. J. Wickham,
  list of authorities, 8.
  Westminster Inventory, 60n.
Lent cloth or veil, 52.
Leryffax, William, 44n.
Leverton,
  chrismatory, 46n.
  elevation curtain, 26.
  tucking girdle, 59n.
Lewanick, 53.
Library, 45n.
Lights, 19, 20, 29, 31, 44, 50, 51, 53.
Lincoln Minster, 38n, 41n.
Lion at rogation procession, 54.
Litany desk, 48.
Little Casterton, 41n.
Lofts, 42.
Long Clawson classical stone altar, 22n.
Long Melford, 23n.
  altar cover, 26n.
Long Sutton, 40.
Lord's Table, 39n.

Maldon, Thomas, 31n.
Maniple, 60, 34.
Margaret Pattens, St.
  Lent cross, 37n.
  Paschal bason, 54n.
  Staves for canopy, 51n.
  Tapestry, 27n.
Margaret's, St. Westminster,
  coffer for high altar, 29.
  paste, 43.
  pulpit, 40n.
Martin, Roger, 23n.
Mary-at-Hill, St.,
  altar shelf, 24.
  stools for rectors, 44n.

Mary Wolnoth, St.
  basons, 39n.
Mattersey, 46n.
Melford, 23n, 26n.
Mensa Domini, 39n.
Meppershall, 30n.
Merton College, Oxford, 45n.
Michael, Cornhill, St.
  elevation curtain, 27n.
  foot cloth, 27n.
Milton Abbas, 36n.
Ministerium, 41.
Minor altars, 22.
Miracles, 'feigned,' 21.
Misericorde, 43.
Monstrance, 37, 34.
Moon to bear the Sacrament, 38n.
Morley, 33n.
Morse for cope, 60.
Mortars, 58.

Napkin for baptism, 46.
Nether frontal, 26.
  to be found by parish, 21n.
Newark, 23n.
Nicholas, St. Bishop, 61.
Norwich, St. Leonard's, 30n.

Ooster, 37.
Order of Communion, 19, 31, 33.
Organ, 43.
Ottery St. Mary, 56.
Oundle, 40.

Palla, 33.
  of pasteboard, 34.
Pall for funerals, 50.
  on grave, 51.
Palms, on Palm Sunday, 18.
Palm Sunday, 37.
Paraphrase of Erasmus, 20, 45.
Parish, what it had to provide, 21n.
Parker, J. H. 25n.
Parliament, authority of, 15, 42.
Partrishow, rere tos at, 23n.
Paschal candlestick, 54.
  bason for, 54n.
  post, 53n.
  to be found by parish, 21n.
Puste, 48.
Paston, John, 50n.
Patener, 35.
Paten, 33.
Paul's, St. Ecclesiological Society, 7.
Pax, pax board, 38, 36n.
  to be found by parish, 21n.
Peckham, Archbishop, 28.
Percyval, Sir John, 39n.
Peter's, Cheap, St.,
  elevation curtain, 26.
Peter's, Cornhill, St.,
  lanterns, 58n.
  surplices, 61n.

INDEX.

Pews, 44.
Pictures, 21, 19.
Piscina, 40.
  for font, 46n.
  in floor, 41n.
Plumbetts, 30n.
Poor man's box, 44.
Portugal, reservation in, 29n.
Post, the paschal, 54n.
Presbytery, 41.
Preston, John, 36n.
Pulpit, 45, 20.
Pulpitum, 42.
Purse to carry the pyx, 49.
Pyx, hanging, 49, 28, 34, 37.
  processional, 37.
  standing, 34.
  to be found by parish, 21n.
Pyx cloth, 28.

Quires, 28, 32, 40, 41, 42, 43, 61.
  rulers of the, 44.

Ranworth, reredos at, 23n.
Rationale, 60.
Ravensthorpe, John, 33n.
Raynold, Walter, Abp. 31n.
Reading,
  elevation curtain, 26.
  holy bush, 41n.
  paschal bason, 54n.
  paste, 49.
  reredos, 63.
  standards, 33n.
Reading pulpit, 40.
Register or book mark, 36.
Relics, 19, 22n, 32n.
  not necessary for consecration of altars, 22n.
Reliquary, 32, 34.
Reredos, 23, 24, 26, 63.
Riddels, 27.
Ridley, Bishop of London, destroys altars, 22.
Ripon Minster,
  lenten veil, 52n.
  pyx, 29n.
Rochet, 61.
  to be found by parish, 21n.
Romsey Abbey, 24.
Rood, 42.
  loft, 42.
  organ stood there, 43.
  screen, 42.
Rouen, 57.
Rowell, 44.
Rubric, ornaments, 7, 13, 14.
Russell, Richard, 22n.

Sackering bell, 36.
  to be found by parish, 21n.
Sacrament house, 27, 28, 58.
  lamps before, 29.

Sacrarium, 40.
Salt at baptism, 46.
Sandwich,
  cross of silver, 30n.
  many candles at, 32n.
  pyx, 49.
Sarum in 1222, 34n.
  dedication crosses, 56.
  lenten veil, 52n.
  processional, 54n, 55n.
  use, 37n.
Scarborough, St. Mary's,
  basons, 35n.
Scarf, black, 59.
Scotland, 29n.
Screen, 42.
Seculus, 41, 30n.
Selby, Agnes de, 39n.
Sepulchre at Easter, 52, 27n, 29n.
Seven sacraments on font, 36n.
Shell not used at baptism, 46.
Sherborne, 25.
Shillington, 52n.
Ship for incense, 35.
Shrine, 19, 38.
Shriving cloth, 47.
Shriving pew, 47.
  house, 47.
  stool, 47.
Sidbury, 58n.
Simpson, Rev. Dr. Sparrow, 26n.
Skep for holy bread, 38.
Skins, 27n.
Smeton, Matilda de, 32n.
Southampton, Austin Friars, 29.
Spicer, Maud, 40n.
Spoon for chalice, 33.
  for incense, 35.
Sprinkle for holy water, 38.
Stalls, 43.
Stamford, St. George's, 21n.
Standers, 44, 60.
Standing candlesticks, 33.
"Stations of the Cross," foreign and modern, 22.
Staves for chanters, 43.
Stephen's, St., Coleman St.
  coffins for altars, 24, 29.
  monstrance, 38n.
  prayer books, 45.
  presbytery, 41n.
Stephen's, Walbrook, St.
  altar cover, 26n.
  chafing ball, 57n.
  garlands, 33n.
  Judas candle, 54n.
  organ stool, 43n.
Steyning, 48.
Stole, 59, 60.
Stools, 43.
Stratton, 54n.
Streamers, 54.
Sudary, 34.

Sudbury, 31n.
Sun for Sacrament, 37n.
Super-altar, 35.
Super frontal, 26.
Surplice, 58, 59.
  silk, 61n, 39n.
  to be found by parish, 21n.

Tabernacle, Italian, for Sacrament, 23n.
Table, reredos, 23, 25, 68.
  communion, 23n.
  with inscriptions, 45.
Tadcaster, 46n.
Tallington, 30n.
Tanfield, 47n.
Tapestry, 27.
Textus, 32.
Thornes, crucifix at, 22n.
Tilbrook, 46n.
Tippel, 59.
Tonstal, 48n.
Torches, 36, 37n, 50, 51.
Torch staves, 51.
Towells, altar cloths, 39.
  lavatory, 35.
  to be found by parish, 21n.
Trendle, 44.
Trendyl for a towell, 35n.
Triangular candlestick, 53.
Tucking girdle, 59.
Tunicle, 60, 61.
  to be found by the parish, 21n.

Ut parochiani, 21n, 61n.

Vat for holy water, 38.
  to be found by parish, 21n.
Vail for Lent, 52.
  to be found by parish, 21n.
Verger, 55.
Vertame (canopy for processions), 51n.
Vestment, 60.
  to be found by parish, 21n.
Vestry girdle, 60n.
Vestry library, 45n.

Wakefield, crucifix at, 22n.
  fireplace, 57n.
  stone altar at, 22n, 25n.
Wulberswick, 28n.
Walpole, St. Andrew's, 46n.
Wands, 55, 44.
Wandsworth, 47n.
Wartree, Richard, 33n.
Watching closet, 47n.
Wedding gear, 48, 49.
Weights of lead, 30n, 36n.
Welborne, John, 38n.
West Grinstead, 28n.
West Meston, 31n.
Westminster Abbey, altars at, 23n, 25n.
  frontal at, 26n.
  monstrance, 38n.
  St. Stephen's, 46n.
White branches, 50.
  canons, 41.
Wiggenhale St. Peter, 46n.
Winchelsea, Robert, Abp., 61.
Winchester, altar rails, 23n.
  chapel in, 26n.
  pyx canopy, 28n.
Wing, 31n, 51n.
Wykeham, William of, 20n.

York, wooden altar, 22n.
  bills for name, 33n.
  box for breads, 34n.
  chalice spoon, 33n.
  copes for standers, 44n.
  cross at funeral, 50n.
  cushions at high altar, 32n.
  images, 32n.
  mass book, 37n.
  plumbets, 30n.
  Pontificals, 55n, 56n.
  Rowyll, 44.
  silver bacons, 35n.
  torch, 36n.
  tunicles, 61n.

Xanten 63n.

THE ALCUIN CLUB.

Chairman.
J. WICKHAM LEGG, Esq. F.S.A.

Committee.

W. J. BIRKBECK, Esq., M.A. F.S.A.
H. B. BRIGGS, Esq.
Rev. F. E. BRIGHTMAN, M.A.
Rev. A. L. COATES, M.A.
J. N. COMPER, Esq.
LELAND L. DUNCAN, Esq. F.S.A.
Rev. W. HOWARD FRERE, M.A.
W. H. St. JOHN HOPE, Esq. M.A.
Rev. W. H. H. JERVOIS, M.A.
Rev. T. A. LACEY, M.A.
J. T. MICKLETHWAITE, Esq. F.S.A.
Rev. G. H. PALMER, B.A.
ATHELSTAN RILEY, Esq. M.A.
Rev. H. A. WILSON, M.A.
Rev. CHR. WORDSWORTH, M.A.

Hon. Secretary and Treasurer.
A. E. MAIDLOW DAVIS, Esq. 91a Billiter Buildings, London, E.C.

There existed already in London three Societies, the Henry Bradshaw Society for editing rare Liturgical Texts, the Plainsong and Mediæval Music Society, and St. Paul's Ecclesiological Society, for dealing with liturgical and musical subjects, and with ecclesiology in general; but there was no Society which dealt with the practical study of ceremonial, or the arrangement of churches, their furniture, and ornaments, in accordance with the rubrics of the Book of Common Prayer. To encourage this study the Alcuin Club was formed, which, although practical, is intended to work upon purely historical, and of course, English, lines. Strict obedience to the Book of Common Prayer is the guiding principle of the work of the Club.

[P.T.O.

The Club has already published the following tracts:

"**The Ornaments of the Rubric**" by J. T. MICKLETHWAITE, F.S.A.

"**Consolidation,**" by the Rev. W. C. E. NEWBOLT, M.A. Canon Residentiary of St. Paul's.

And as soon as its funds permit, the Club will publish other Tracts, and Works containing illustrations from miniatures and other ancient examples, on the following subjects:

"**Liturgical Interpolations**" by the Rev. T. A. LACEY (*in the Press.*)

"**The English Altar**" (a series of collotypes: with illustrative text.)

"**The Ornaments of the Ministers.**"

"**The Liturgical Colours.**"

"**The Ornaments of the Altar.**"

"**A Celebration of the Eucharist with only one Minister.**"

"**The Divine Service.**"

"**Chancels as in times past.**"

"**The Burial Service.**"

"**The Marriage Service,**" &c., &c.

The Club consists of *Members* and *Associates*, who must be in communion with the Church of England.

The Subscription for *Members* is £1. a year, entitling them to all publications *gratis*; and for *Associates* five shillings a year, entitling them to such of the Tracts *gratis*, and to such reductions on other publications as the Committee may determine.

www.ingramcontent.com/pod-product-compliance
Lightning Source LLC
Chambersburg PA
CBHW020242090426
42735CB00010B/1794